What Others Are Saying About This Book:

"Dear Rev. Malkmus: Your book *Why Christians Get Sick* is terrific!"

—Dr. Nathan M. Meyer, President, Bible Prophecy Association, Ohio

"I am overjoyed that your voice with the truth about keeping healthy is being heard in the Christian community. The Christian Booksellers Convention just ended here in Atlanta. Usually someone selects a 'Book of the Year'.... [I believe that your book, *Why Christians Get Sick*] deserves to be honored as 'Book of the Century'!"

—Janet Bryan, Georgia

"I have just finished reading the book *Why Christians Get Sick*. I agree that this is the greatest next to the Bible. It opened my eyes to many things. I had been searching for a book like this for a long time."

—Rev. E.S. Bell, Caraopolis, Pennsylvania

"...Oh, Rev. Malkmus and Rhonda, I admire you for your commitment. God Bless! I have never read such a small book [*Why Christians Get Sick*] with such gigantic content.... How can I become a part of your ministry?"

—Amalia Smith, Puerto Rico

"I have just finished reading your book *Why Christians Get Sick*. You certainly hit the nail on the head, and in such a clear and readable way.... For the last 22 years my husband and I have devoted our lives to helping others know the natural laws of health and ways of healing, not using the drug and surgical methods we once treated our patients with...."

—Dr. Agatha M. Thrash, M.D., Seale, Alabama

"I have just finished reading your book *Why Christians Get Sick* and am greatly encouraged by what you are doing...."

Anthony Wong, Singapore, China

"I just finished reading your book *Why Christians Get Sick* and it has turned my life around. Thank you for such a caring and valuable message...."

—Doris Oldham, South Carolina

"My husband is a pastor and we have two boys, ages 7 and 11. We are home-schoolers also. I have read your book *Why Christians Get Sick* and it has changed our lives...."

—Deborah Boyd, Georgia

"I just finished reading your book *Why Christians Get Sick*. Thank you so much! I see a growing army uniting in this great battle. Please put me on your mailing list...."

—Pastor Don Bressette, Ohio

"[I] have read the book *Why Christians Get Sick*, heard a small audiotape and read three issues of *Back to the Garden*.... Keep up the good work. America, if not the world, needs to hear this message. I believe our hospitals could virtually be emptied by the change in lifestyle."

—Joe Roper, Ohio

"Your book *Why Christians Get Sick* is absolutely fascinating! I could hardly put it down. Thank you so much for sharing your experiences! Also, I very much enjoy your newsletters. These letters along with your programs and seminars provide excellent educational opportunities for anyone interested in good health...."

—Julie Seward, Tennessee

Treasure House

An Imprint of

Destiny Image® Publishers, Inc.
P.O. Box 310
Shippensburg, PA 17257-0310

"For where your treasure is,
there will your heart be also." Matthew 6:21

ISBN 0-7684-2309-0
(previously ISBN 1-56043-849-5 and 0-929619-01-3)
Library of Congress Catalog Card No. 88-81200

For Worldwide Distribution
Printed in the U.S.A.

8 9 10 / 10

This book and all other Destiny Image, Revival Press, MercyPlace, Fresh Bread, Destiny Image Fiction, and Treasure House books are available at Christian bookstores and distributors worldwide.

To order a book, call **1-800-722-6774**.
For more information on foreign distributors, call **717-532-3040**.
Or reach us on the Internet:

www.destinyimage.com

What Others Are Saying About the Diet Recommended by Dr. Malkmus

"We first heard about you on a broadcast that offered your book *Why Christians Get Sick*. Our whole family has adopted the Hallelujah Diet and *life is better for all*!!! Since going on the Hallelujah Diet, my husband Bill has eliminated his heartburn; his hiatal hernia is gone; he has more energy, has lost 16 pounds, and has been able to give up his six to eight Mylanta per day. I (Yvonne) have lost 30 pounds; my migraines are gone; nerves are calmed; panic attacks gone; arthritis in back gone; circulation improved, no more cold and tingling hands and feet; fever blisters gone; spastic colon and hemorrhoids gone; fibrous breast tumors gone; greater physical strength and mental clarity. Our daughter, Amy, who has spina bifida and juvenile diabetes is off antibiotic for her kidneys; reduced insulin from 23 to 4 units a day; lost 14 pounds, and her constipation problem of 19 years is gone. Also, her skin has improved and she has more energy and is stronger. My 74-year-old mother is off her blood pressure medicine; skin much improved and has lost 16 pounds.... Thank you for all that you do to help others."

—Yvonne, Bill, and Amy Roberts, Maryland

"Dear Brother Malkmus... [As a pastor] I have had concerns about people expecting a miracle each time their bodies became sick. [Not] everyone who received prayer...received healing. I have studied the Greek word for healing in the New Testament for clarity of meaning but something was missing until a friend of ours told us about your book *Why Christians Get Sick*. As I read this book, I felt that the answers I had been seeking were right before my eyes. I have always contended that the Word of God contained everything we needed for all portions of our lives if we could just come to the correct knowledge of it, as you refer to in Hosea '*my people are destroyed for lack of knowledge*.' I have had information given to me about lifestyle changes from a nutritional viewpoint before, but your relating it to the Scriptures got my attention!

...Thank you for writing *Why Christians Get Sick* and *God's Way to Ultimate Health....*"

—Pastor Louis Boyd, Texas

WHY CHRISTIANS GET SICK

DR. GEORGE H. MALKMUS

That Thy way may be known upon earth, Thy saving health among all nations (Psalm 67:2).

For I will restore health unto thee, and I will heal thee of thy wounds, saith the Lord… (Jeremiah 30:17).

Bless the Lord, O my soul: and all that is within me, bless His holy name. Bless the Lord, O my soul, and forget not all His benefits: Who forgiveth all thine iniquities; who healeth all thy diseases; who redeemeth thy life from destruction; who crowneth thee with lovingkindness and tender mercies; who satisfieth thy mouth with good things; so that thy youth is renewed like the eagles (Psalm 103:1-5).

ACKNOWLEDGMENTS

I wish to acknowledge the wonderful help of those who offered suggestions, provided materials, made oodles of corrections, did proofreading, and constantly encouraged me. Without their help and encouragement, this book would not have been possible!

Michelle Austin

Jack and Carol Barber

Carolyn Cocks

Robert and Judith Carballo

Rev. Paul Dow

Rev. and Mrs. Glen Hamilton

Bill and Helen Luce

Janet Malkmus

Marge Porterfield

Rev. David E. Strong

My sincere appreciation to Wayne Allen for the cover design.

CONTENTS

INTRODUCTION

Each year, approximately 25,000 people die on the highways of America because of alcohol! Because of the personal loss of loved ones, Mothers Against Drunk Driving (MADD) was established to enlighten the American people to the dangers of drinking and driving. Certainly alcohol is a scourge on the American people and I applaud all who try to expose this carnage and reduce alcohol-related deaths and injuries.

However, there is another scourge in America. Only this one is taking the lives of millions of Americans each year and over half of them are Christians! Yet there seems to be no voice or organized effort crying out against this unnecessary loss of millions of lives, many who are dying in the very prime of life!

Each year, over one million Americans die from heart disease while over a half-million die from cancer! Most of these deaths are absolutely unnecessary! But why are there no voices crying out against this needless waste of lives and exposing this carnage?

The obvious answer to that question is that most people do not realize that sickness and disease are not necessary and can be avoided! Yes, heart disease, cancer, stroke, diabetes, and a host of other diseases can be eliminated if Christians will return to the Bible and observe the natural laws God gave man thousands of years ago!

This book delves into the question of *Why Christians Get Sick* and then goes on to give the biblical answer! Yes, this book tells how Christians can avoid sickness and disease while experiencing superior health!

As Mothers Against Drunk Driving (MADD) united to expose the unnecessary loss of life through alcohol, so must Christians arise and unite to expose the unnecessary loss of millions of lives to heart disease, cancer, stroke, diabetes, etc., each year! May God raise up multitudes of Christian warriors to expose this scourge!

This book will help you to understand the problem as well as the solution! May God bless you...open your eyes...illuminate your mind...and help you to understand as you read! Then, with knowledge, love, and the power of God, may we go forth united to help others understand *Why Christians Get Sick* and show them how they too can avoid sickness and disease and experience superior health!

FOREWORD

‹═══──◦──═══›

C an you spare a few hours of your valuable time? You can read this book in just a few hours, and those few hours could change your life!

There are many good books on "health" available today. But few tell us what God's Word has to say about it! My friend and fellow-preacher of the gospel, Rev. George H. Malkmus, has done this in his book *Why Christians Get Sick*. He, as you will read, is living proof that practicing God's principles of health does remove sickness and provide energy and desire to serve God faithfully, all the days of our lives.

This book is God's answer to the pantheistic "holistic health" that is increasingly being absorbed into the "New Age Movement." Please consider the Scriptures presented and prayerfully make them a part of your life. Be a "noble Berean" and "see if these things be so!"

I became interested in the scriptural principles of this book when I, as a pastor, was visiting and listening to the woes of the sick, with their health and money gone; they were eating more pills than food and were scared and bewildered. I contrasted their bitter end with that of the Old Testament fathers who "Gathered up [their] feet into the bed, and yielded up the ghost, and [were] gathered unto [their] people" (Gen. 49:33). They had all their mental faculties, were apparently without sickness or pain, and peacefully, joyfully, went home to be with the Lord. Some contrast!

Is it possible to escape the pain, astronomical medical bills, and loss of our faculties experienced by the majority of us and, instead, be energetic, productive, and happy until God takes us home? Yes! Yes!! Yes!!!

My prayers join the author's that you, dear reader, will read the book, study the Scripture presented, heed the testimonies and admonitions, and reap the benefits in your and others' lives! May God guide you as you read!

Rev. David E. Strong
Wilmington, New York

CHAPTER 1

MY DILEMMA

———⊰•⊱———

My people are destroyed for lack of knowledge (Hosea 4:6).

Joe was a friend, a big powerful man who had been an All-American football tackle. He was also a very successful evangelist who was being mightily used by the Lord. He had held several revivals for me through the years in various churches that I pastored. I always looked forward to Joe being with us. He was a very kind, helpful, spiritual man with whom I enjoyed good fellowship.

In a message to the church during one of these revivals, Joe said, "I believe that over 90% of all sickness among Christians is because of sin!" Being a young, impressionable preacher, I, too, while preaching, would say on occasion, "I believe that over 90% of all sickness among Christians is because of sin!"

We kept in touch through the years. Not many years later I received a letter from Joe requesting prayer. His need? He had suffered a heart attack and was lying in a hospital bed unable to preach scheduled revivals. Being a very well-known evangelist in great demand, he usually stayed fully booked for years in advance.

Along with his letter, Joe had included a photograph of himself lying in the hospital bed.

After I had read the letter and looked at the photo, my first reaction was, "Could this heart attack be because of sin? Had Joe fallen out of favor with God?" This physical problem that my Christian brother was experiencing troubled me greatly because I knew what a great work he had been doing for the Lord. Also, we had prayed together on many occasions, and I knew of his total commitment to the work of the Lord and the many personal sacrifices he was making in his dedication to full-time evangelism.

Christian Leader Suffers Stroke

Then it happened again not too many years later to another Christian leader for whom I had the utmost respect—a man among men. This outstanding Christian, who was also an evangelist and the founder of a large Christian youth camp, experienced a stroke that left him partially paralyzed.

Christians all over the world were asked to pray, but his ministry was curtailed sharply, and after several additional strokes, he died. Could these strokes and the untimely death of this great Christian leader be the result of sin? Was his death the will of God? It seems the stock answer among Christians when something like this happens is often, "It must have been God's will."

Christian Publisher Has Heart Attack

Shortly thereafter, another evangelist and publisher of a great Christian periodical that boldly stood for the fundamentals of the faith suffered a heart attack. Christians and churches from all over the world once again were asked to pray, but after a continuing deterioration in his health, he also died. Was his death because of sin? Could it be that the death of this greatly used man of God was the will of God?

Founder of Christian College Suffers From Senility

At about the same time another Christian leader, also an evangelist and the founder of one of the best-known Christian universities in America, was having a terrible problem with senility. His senility was so severe that for many years before his death he was unable to function or have any kind of ministry. Could his senility be the result of sin? Could it be that this senility was the will of God?

By this time, I was extremely troubled at what I was seeing happen to men I respected, men I looked up to as the great spiritual leaders of the day. God had even used some of these men when He called me into the ministry.

Christian Missionary Dies From Cancer

Of all the troubling experiences I went through, the most upsetting up to this time was something that happened at a preachers' conference around the year 1974. The church I was pastoring had been kind enough to send me to the conference for rest and refreshment. It was a time to fellowship with other preachers and to get my spiritual batteries recharged. However, I returned from this conference more perplexed and troubled than ever.

There were over 1,200 preachers from all over the world attending this conference. Toward the end of the conference, the host pastor presented a missionary pastor to the gathered preachers. He was pastoring a church of some 15,000 people in the Philippines and was experiencing fantastic blessings in his ministry. However, he had been forced to leave this ministry because of cancer. At only 45 years of age, the doctors had given him only a few months to live.

We had special prayer for him. Over 1,200 preachers prayed for his healing. After we had collective prayer, we were encouraged to take this prayer request back to our respective churches also to pray for his healing. This represented the potential of having more than 100,000 Christians praying for this evangelist to get well and be able to return to the field where he was doing such a mighty work for the Lord. But he did not get well. In fact, he died not very long thereafter. Could his death have been the result of sin? If his death was not because of sin, then why didn't the Lord answer the prayers of this multitude of Christians who were praying for his healing? Was his death the will of God? These were hard questions and they bothered me greatly, as there just did not seem to be any answer that made sense. These were questions that I, as a pastor, felt I should know the answers to…but I didn't!

I am sharing only some of the most outstanding examples because all during these years I was seeing just ordinary, lesser-known Christians, as well as members of the various churches I was pastoring, experiencing numerous physical problems and seemingly untimely deaths. Many of my preacher friends also had physical ailments as well, some that were serious enough to hinder their ministries. Some of them had even died!

Now It Was My Turn

It was in 1976, however, that this whole perplexing problem of sickness among Christians came to a climax. Six years earlier I had started a new church in upstate New York. The church had grown from just my own family in the beginning to a membership of over 600. Some were driving in excess of 100 miles to attend our services. Many were coming to know the Lord Jesus as their personal Savior.

We were broadcasting on three radio stations each week and had five large buses on the road bringing people to Sunday school and church services. There was a printing ministry and a bookstore ministry. Our Christian school had over 100 students in kindergarten through grade 12, along with a Bible Institute. Our Christian school was ranked as one of the top five Christian schools in the nation. Over a dozen of our young people were in Christian colleges, some preparing for full-time Christian work. None could deny that the Lord's blessing was on this ministry.

Then it happened! With all of these wonderful blessings going on in my own ministry, in 1976, at the age of 42, I was told that I had colon cancer, along with some other serious physical problems. Wow! This was mind-boggling! Could this sickness be because of "sin" in my own life? Was this the will of God for me? As I look back on it even to this day, I don't know how I could have been more sincere or dedicated to the Lord and His work. To say the least, this was very devastating to me.

This all happened only a short time after I had watched my own mother die as a result of cancer, following many years of medical treatment. Her illness and deterioration was a terrible thing to have to witness. I believe Mom suffered more from the treatments she received than she did from the cancer itself.

After watching my own mother go through this terrible ordeal, I was determined not to follow the conventional cancer treatments for my own body. So I searched for and found an alternative: nutrition and a changed lifestyle! It had worked for others, but there was no assurance that it would work for me. However, I felt it was at least an alternative that made sense and that did not contradict the teaching of the Bible, as did the administering of drugs.

I Leave the Ministry

So I left the ministry and moved to a small town in Florida. There, I attended classes at a nutritional institute, as well as put into practice the things that were being taught. Almost immediately unbelievable things started to happen in my body. Not only did the serious problems start to go away but even minor problems started to make their exit from my body as well. To say the least, it was very, very exciting. But I will talk more about this in a later chapter.

My Dilemma

Even more exciting than the healing I was experiencing in my own body was what I saw happening in the lives of others who were also at this nutritional institute. People were there from all over the world with all kinds of physical complaints. Many of these people were not professing Christians. Some of them were openly agnostic. Yet, when they applied the principles that were being taught, truly miraculous healing took place and they got well.

Now I was really faced with a dilemma. For nearly 20 years while in the Christian ministry, I watched Christians get sick and often die from a variety of illnesses in spite of many prayers and the efforts of the medical profession. Now I was faced with personally witnessing even non-Christians getting well without prayer, the medical profession, or even acknowledging God in their lives. How was I to account for this? The rest of this book, *Why Christians Get Sick*, is devoted to answering this most important question.

Chapter 1—In Review

Before we continue, let me think about this subject of sickness among Christians and ask some questions to stimulate our thinking:

1. Could it be possible that Christians are too passive when it comes to sickness, accepting and enduring sickness without resistance?

2. Could the reason for Christian passivity be because we are fatalistic in our thinking?

3. Could it be possible that we are attributing sickness to "sin" or "the will of God" when, in reality, the cause of that sickness might be the violation of some natural laws of God?

4. Have you ever wondered why Christians are just as sick as non-Christians? Or why spiritual Christians are just as sick as Christians who are not as spiritual?

5. Could it be possible that Christians don't have to experience heart attacks, strokes, cancer, senility, diabetes, and a host of other ailments including colds, flu, headaches, sinuses, allergies, pimples, tooth decay, arthritis, etc.?

6. Could it be that Christians don't want to acknowledge the possibility that perhaps something they are doing (or not doing) is responsible for their illness? (Blaming instead some outside force, such as germs, heredity, viruses, fate, God, etc.)

7. Could it be possible that Christians are getting sick and dying untimely deaths because *"My people are destroyed for lack of knowledge"* (Hos. 4:6)?

CHAPTER 2

I AM FEARFULLY AND
WONDERFULLY MADE

———➤◦◄———

I will praise Thee; for I am fearfully and wonderfully made:
marvelous are Thy works; and that my soul knoweth right well
(Psalm 139:14).

I believe that God created man! I do not believe that man's
existence is the result of some evolutionary process! For
just as a watch, which is so intricately made, must have a
watchmaker, man, who is so much more intricately made, had to
have a Maker!

I also believe that the Bible is the very "Word of God"; that
God not only created man, but also had a book of instructions written: "*All scripture is given by inspiration of God, and is profitable...*"
(2 Tim. 3:16). This book of instructions, the Bible, contains all that
God the Creator wanted man, His creation, to know! Yes, all that
men needed to know in order to live a healthy, happy, successful,
spiritual life is found in the pages of the Bible!

The Bible answers the three basic questions of man. Namely:

1. "Where did man come from?"

2. "Why is he here?"

3. "Where is he going when his life here on earth is over?"

In this chapter, we must lay some groundwork so that in later chapters we may fully understand why Christians get sick.

Where Did Man Come From?

The Bible says, *"In the beginning, God created the heaven and the earth"* (Gen. 1:1). Then the Bible goes on in Genesis chapter 1 to explain the six days of creation.

Day One: God created light (see Gen. 1:3-5).

Day Two: God created vapor above and water below (see Gen. 1:6-8).

Day Three: God created land, sea, and plant life (see Gen. 1:9-13).

Day Four: God created sun, moon, and stars (see Gen. 1:14-19).

Day Five: God created animal life (see Gen. 1:20-23).

Day Six: God created cattle and humans (see Gen. 1:24-31).

Let's examine the sixth day of creation more carefully, as it is extremely relevant to the understanding of why Christians get sick.

First, let's see how the Bible says that God made man: *"And the Lord God formed man of the dust of the ground, and breathed into his nostrils the breath of life: And man became a living soul"* (Gen. 2:7).

When the Bible states, *"I am fearfully and wonderfully made,"* truer words were never spoken. Our body is literally a chemical factory, composed of almost every element in the mineral kingdom. Listing only the major elements, man is composed of: oxygen (65%), carbon (15%), hydrogen (10%), nitrogen (3%), calcium (2%), phosphorus (1%), along with trace amounts of sulfur, sodium, chlorine, fluorine, potassium, magnesium, iron, silicon, iodine, copper, lead, aluminum, etc.

From the above, it is clear to see that man is made up primarily of the airborne elements ("breath of life"), while the remaining elements come from the earth ("dust of the ground"), about 4%. The Bible repeatedly confirms that God used these building materials in the making of man. "*In the sweat of thy face shalt thou eat bread, till thou return unto the ground; for out of it wast thou taken; for dust thou art, and unto dust shalt thou return*" (Gen. 3:19). See also Psalm 103:14 and Ecclesiastes 12:7.

So here we have a book, written thousands of years ago, telling us the building material of which man is made: the "dust of the ground" and "breath of life." These statements of the Bible are confirmed by the most modern of scientific findings—that man is, indeed, made of the elements contained in the earth and air. How can anyone doubt the Bible as being anything but the very "Word of God"? Science has only recently discovered what the Bible has been telling us for millennia!

100 Trillion Cells

This body of ours consists of about 100,000,000,000,000 (100 trillion) cells, which require constant nourishment for rebuilding. These cells also require constant cleansing of contaminants. Some parts of the body are renewed as often as every week or so; much of the body is rebuilt every year; while the bones (or the skeleton) require as much as several years for total rebuilding and replacement.

If these cells are not provided with the proper building materials, and the cells are not kept cleansed of toxic material, progressively weaker cells will replace the strong cells with which we were born. These weaker cells eventually result in sickness, tooth decay, poor eyesight, loss of hearing, baldness, senility, cancer, as well as a host of other physical problems, and ultimately, an early or untimely death.

When people start to experience these and other breakdowns in their bodies, they usually attribute the breakdown to heredity, getting older, or often in the case of many Christians: "the will of God." They never seem to realize that these problems are the direct result of failing to provide the body's cells with proper and adequate nourishment. Proper nourishment is absolutely essential for the replenishment of the cells, so that new cells will be as strong or stronger than those they are replacing. Nor do people realize that their lifestyle and diets have polluted their bodies—bodies so full of poisons that the cells are literally being drowned in these pollutants. Thus, we see that the health and condition of the cells determine the health and condition of the entire body.

The Blood

The human body, depending on size, has approximately five quarts of blood, which are constantly traveling through the entire body, making 3,000 to 5,000 round-trips a day! The heart pumps some 20,000,000,000 (20 billion) blood cells throughout the body. These blood cells carry nourishment to the body cells, while collecting wastes to be removed from the body.

The heart muscle must be kept strong in order to keep the blood continuously moving with good strength as it feeds and cleanses the body cells. Many people fail to realize the absolute necessity of aerobic exercises for the maintaining of a strong heart to pump the blood.

The Lungs

The respiratory system (lungs) works together with the circulatory system (heart, arteries, veins, and blood) as the life support system of the body. The body can go 40-plus days without food, possibly 4 days without water, but less than 4 minutes without air (oxygen).

The lungs take in oxygen and give off carbon dioxide. The oxygen is picked up by the blood and taken to every part of the body where it becomes food for the building of new cells. On its return trip, it picks up the garbage—carbon dioxide and other toxins—and returns them to the lungs for removal from the body.

It is carbon dioxide that causes soda pop to bubble and fizz. When a person drinks a carbonated drink, little do they realize they are dumping a toxic substance into their body.

If the oxygen supply is restricted by a clogged artery to the brain, a stroke results. If that restriction is to the heart, a heart attack is the result. Our lifestyle and diet determine the condition of our lungs, arteries, veins, etc., and the availability of oxygen to the cells.

Breathing polluted air and smoking are like committing slow suicide! Every breath of these pollutants shortens the life of that individual.

The Liver

The liver takes every particle of food we eat and everything we drink into its marvelous laboratory and breaks it down into a usable form. The blood then takes this specially prepared food to the various parts of the body to repair, replenish, and rebuild cells and tissues.

Alcohol, beer, wine, and liquor slowly destroy this marvelous organ, which ultimately results in serious physical problems and untimely deaths.

Other Organs

If space permitted, we could talk about the lymph (which we will cover in a later chapter), nerves, muscles, glands, and a host of other parts with which God made man. But I believe we have already shown more than enough to prove the Bible accurate when it states that we are *fearfully and wonderfully made.*

Chapter 2—In Review

At the conclusion of each chapter, we will review some of the most important things we have learned:

1. God made man from the elements found in the dust and in the air!

2. Scientific evidence confirms that man's body is, indeed, comprised of the elements found in soil and air.

3. The body consists of trillions of cells that are in a constant state of being replaced.

4. Proper building materials are absolutely necessary for the building of strong, healthy, vibrant cells.

5. The blood constantly transports these building materials from the liver and lungs to every part of the body.

6. If any part of the body lacks health and efficient function, it is because the building materials brought by the blood have been unsuitable or inadequate for the purpose of maintaining health, and/or the body is polluted with poisons.

7. The only source from which the blood can derive the building materials for the rebuilding of cells is from the food we eat, the liquid we drink, and the air we breathe.

CHAPTER 3

BIBLICAL REASONS

—➤◦◄—

For this cause many are weak and sickly among you, and many sleep (1 Corinthians 11:30).

Have you ever wondered, "Why are Christians just as sick as non-Christians?" Or, "Why are spiritual Christians just as sick as Christians who are not as spiritual?" These two questions were asked at the conclusion of Chapter 1 of this book. But they are two questions that greatly bothered me for many years while pastoring various churches.

As I mentioned in Chapter 1, I have seen great Christian leaders—evangelists, missionaries, and pastors—get sick and even die, some in the prime of life, doing great works for the Lord. I have also seen Christians get cancer, have heart attacks, upset stomachs, and you name it, just like non-Christians. As Christians, how can we account for this?

What Various Religions Teach

Different religions, Christian denominations, and their proponents have had some very interesting teachings and practices concerning sickness. Let's look at some of them:

Christian Science (founded by Mary Baker Glover Patterson Eddy) teaches that sickness and death are not real, only mental error. Yet the founder of this religion, as well as multitudes of its followers (including one of my own aunts who was a Christian Scientist), got sick and died.

Seventh-Day Adventists (whose group was founded by Ellen G. White) have included in the teachings of their religion some very strict teachings on diet and care of the body. For instance, they teach against the use of coffee, tea, tobacco, and alcoholic beverages. One of the more interesting teachings is that they are to eat no pork and that it is best to eat no meat at all. Though the followers of this religion have not all followed these dietary teachings, statistics show that Adventists have less incidence of cancer and, in general, are healthier than the average American. Further, as a group they live six years longer than the average American.

Mormons (whose religion was founded by Joseph Smith) also include dietary restrictions in their teachings. These include abstaining from the use of alcohol, tobacco, coffee, tea, cola, and other substances containing a drug. They also encourage the storage of emergency food...especially grains and pure drinking water.

Pentecostals generally teach that healing of the body was included in the atonement. They often have healing services and healing lines at which time they may apply oil along with prayers for healing. I have personally been in meetings where they demanded God to heal the affliction in the "name of Jesus." But in some 20 years of ministry, coming in contact with many Pentecostal pastors and their parishioners, I have not seen any less frequency of sickness among their group.

Baptists (and I was a Baptist pastor for almost 20 years) are often extremely fatalistic when it comes to sickness. They pray very sincerely and they accept treatment with drugs, radiation, and surgery by the medical profession as a means that God uses to heal Christians who are sick. If prayers and the efforts of the medical profession don't bring healing, then that sickness is accepted as the "will of God." But in over 30 years of association with Baptists, I have not seen them, as a group, to have any better health than non-Baptists.

Is God to Blame?

I have not included the above review for the purpose of being unkind. However, I believe that it is high time we stopped hiding behind the Lord and blaming Him for our physical problems. And that is exactly what we are doing most of the time when we say that it's God's will when sickness comes to us, a friend, or one of our loved ones.

It seems that we tend to blame things we do not understand on the Lord. For instance, a tornado devastates a town in Oklahoma; or a hurricane rips the coast of Louisiana; or floods inundate a certain community. In each of these incidents, human lives are lost and there is great property damage. Who gets the blame for these tragedies? Why, "it was an act of God" according to the insurance company or the news commentator. What they are actually saying is, "God is to blame!"

Let's stop blaming God for things we don't understand! And let's turn to the Bible and see what the Lord has to tell us about this subject of sickness among Christians…just why do Christians get sick?

The Bible gives only three reasons for sickness or physical problems among Christians, and I believe that every physical affliction suffered by Christians today falls into one of these three categories.

I. For the Glory of God

In the Gospel of John, chapter 9, verses 1-3, we read of a man who was blind from birth. Neither he nor his parents had sinned. The Bible asks: "Who did sin, this man or his parents, that he was born blind?" Jesus answered, "Neither hath this man sinned, nor his parents: but that the works of God should be made manifest in him."

It is very clear that this incident happened while Jesus was on this earth and that this blindness was for a purpose: so that Jesus could heal him, thus calling attention to Himself, who He was, and to the Father who sent Him!

The apostle Paul seemed to have a physical affliction that would fit into this category. Paul prayed three times for healing but the Lord said in Second Corinthians 12:7-9: "*My grace is sufficient for thee*."

If this is our lot, and we have a sickness for the glory of God, then we must learn to say as Paul did, "*For I have learned, in what-soever state I am, therewith to be content*" (Phil. 4:11). All the praying in the world will not remove an affliction that is for the glory of God.

II. Because of Unconfessed Sin

In First Corinthians 11:28-32 we read about weakness, sickness, and an early death coming upon believers when they would not confess their sins, and God had to judge them. "*For this cause many are weak and sickly among you, and many sleep. For if we would judge ourselves, we should not be judged. But when we are judged, we are chastened of the Lord, that we should not be condemned with the world*" (1 Cor. 11:30-32).

Sickness because of sin is a judgment by the Lord, but it can be removed if we make things right with the Lord. Reread First Corinthians 11:30-32 in this regard. And by the way, all the praying in the world will not heal the affliction caused by sin, unless it is the prayer of repentance by the believer who has sinned!

I have no doubt that some of the physical suffering among Christians of our day is because of unconfessed sin. However, I believe that the physical sufferings of this group comprise a very small percentage of today's physical problems.

Today if a Christian is experiencing a physical problem, it is easy enough to find out if the sickness is because of sin...sincere forgiveness (see 1 John 1:9). If this doesn't bring healing, then the sickness is almost certainly due to the third reason the Bible gives for sickness: the violation of God's natural laws!

III. The Violation of God's Natural Laws

In First Corinthians 3:16-17 we read, *"Know ye not that ye are the temple of God, and that the spirit of God dwelleth in you? If any man defile the temple of God, him shall God destroy; for the temple of God is holy, which temple ye are."*

These Scriptures puzzled me for many years. It was not until I personally had physical problems, which resulted in my studying how the body functions and in learning the importance of proper nutrition and vigorous exercise, that my eyes were opened to what the Bible was teaching here in First Corinthians 3:16-17.

There is additional teaching on this subject in First Corinthians 6:19-20: *"What? know ye not that your body is the temple of the Holy Ghost which is in you, which ye have of God, and ye are not your own? For ye are bought with a price: therefore glorify God in your body, and in your spirit, which are God's."*

Clearly, the Bible teaches that the Christian's body is not his own...it belongs to God! If a Christian fails to care properly for his body, God will destroy that body! Let's read that Scripture again: *"If any man defile* ['make unclean with something unpleasant or contaminating'—Webster] *the temple of God, him shall God destroy"* (1 Cor. 3:17).

Our Lack of Knowledge

Most people never give a second thought as to what they put into their mouth. If it tastes good, they eat it. They never seem to associate their physical condition with what they eat or drink. If people were to read the ingredients on the labels before putting things into their mouths, they would be amazed at what they are consuming—substances they often can't even pronounce, much less know what they are! The average person uses more care in selecting the grade of gasoline to put into their automobiles than they do the food they put in their mouth.

Nor do people normally associate the exercise their body receives (or fails to receive) as having anything to do with their physical health. The Bible says we are *"destroyed for lack of knowledge"* (Hos. 4:6).

Purpose for This Writing Book

My purpose for writing this book is to share with you, my Christian brother or sister, some of the knowledge I have obtained and experienced concerning the body and health. Knowledge that, when applied, has literally changed my body and life—I'm now feeling as good or better than I did when I was 20 years old.

Some will heed this knowledge and see marvelous things start to happen within their own bodies. Health will be their portion, and life will take on a new glow. Just feeling so alive will excite you, and living for Jesus will become an increasingly thrilling experience!

Others will reject this knowledge and go on their merry, miserable way to a diseased body, much suffering, and a premature death. *"Be not deceived; God is not mocked: for whatsoever a man soweth, that shall he also reap"* (Gal. 6:7). This Scripture most certainly applies to the subject we have been discussing: "why Christians get sick."

Then there may be someone who says, "But I would rather go to be with Jesus. This world is so wicked, and being with Jesus will be so wonderful, and besides, I'll have a new body." Oh, but you can have a new body here and now if you want it! And let's remember the apostle Paul's words: *"For I am in a strait betwixt two, having a desire to depart, and to be with Christ; which is far better: Nevertheless to abide in the flesh is more needful for you"* (Phil. 1:23-24).

Chapter 3—In Review

1. Christians are just as sick as non-Christians. Spiritual Christians are just as sick as Christians who are not as spiritual. Why?

2. Christians tend to be very fatalistic in their view of sickness, often attributing it to, or even blaming, God for their physical problems.

3. The Bible teaches only three reasons for sickness among Christians:

I. *For the Glory of God*—primarily used in the biblical days to demonstrate the Lord Jesus Christ's power and deity.

II. *Because of Unconfessed Sin by the Christian*—Some of the sickness among Christians today can, no doubt, be attributed to this cause. Repentant prayer will bring healing in this instance.

III. *The Violation of the Natural Laws of God*—It is in this third category that the author believes we will find the cause of over 90% of all Christian sickness and physical suffering being experienced today.

4. Our poor eating habits, lifestyle, and lack of exercise cause most of our physical problems.

5. We do have a choice! Will it be health and happiness or sickness, suffering, and an untimely death? Which will you choose?

CHAPTER 4

TRADITIONAL REASONS

—⊷⊶—

Beware lest any man spoil you through…the tradition of men
(Colossians 2:8).

The lack of knowledge in a particular subject can be devastating…so much so that the Bible says in Hosea 4:6, *"My people are destroyed for lack of knowledge."*
This Scripture was used at the beginning of Chapter 1 where we saw a number of prominent Christians having serious physical problems and untimely deaths. If Christians are having physical problems and experiencing early deaths because of lack of knowledge, this becomes a very serious and tragic matter indeed! For a few moments, let us consider the word *knowledge*, especially as it pertains to Christians.

The Importance of Knowledge

Christians are a very unique group of people. They have personally gained *knowledge* in spiritual matters, resulting in the receiving of Jesus as Savior. This knowledge and the application of this knowledge brings a person out of spiritual darkness into God's marvelous light.

However, this spiritual knowledge that we have can lead us into trouble if we are not careful. Why? Because we have come to know the truth in spiritual matters, we often think we know every-thing about everything, which results in our closing our minds to anything contrary to what we believe, no matter what the subject.

Knowledge is one of the greatest needs of Christians! Jesus spoke about it often. In John 8:32, Jesus said: *"And ye shall **know** the truth, and the truth shall make you free."* And again in John 13:17, *"If you **know** these things, happy are ye if ye do them."*

Need for Open Minds

Christians should have open minds, like the Berean Christians did in Acts 17. I'm not saying we should believe everything, but we should at least listen to it, and then see if it has any validity by checking it against the Word of God. Sadly though, many Christians close their minds to anything different from what their minds are programmed with—often ignorant of the truth, foolish-ly substituting opinions, theories, traditions, and blind belief for *true knowledge.*

Christians (as do non-Christians) often tie themselves to beliefs that were handed down from previous generations, or they hold prejudices picked up along their journey through life. Often these beliefs are false, but the mind is closed to any other opinion. Thus, this closed mind becomes our greatest obstacle to gaining *knowledge* and *truth!* I have even seen Christians reject clear Bible teachings because of having closed minds concerning a particular subject.

Lack of Knowledge Appalling

The lack of *knowledge* concerning why Christians get sick is appalling, and I must admit, I was a star pupil in this ignorance for many, many years. My Christian brother or sister reading this book, will you open your mind enough to at least explore the subject before us? I am not asking you to accept blindly what I am saying in this book, but what I am asking is that you be as open minded as the Berean Christians of Acts 17:11 who *"received the word with all readiness of mind, and searched the scriptures daily whether those things were so."* Will you at least allow your mind to explore the subject? You have nothing to lose except possibly some false beliefs, and you might just swap that old belief for a long healthy, excitingly productive Christian life!

In order to gain *knowledge*, we need to begin by separating what we know to be true from what we have always accepted. We need to separate *true knowledge* from beliefs or opinions.

Traditions

Let's ask a few questions to stimulate our thinking. Why do you eat the way you do? Why do you use a fork and spoon—instead of chopsticks or some other instrument—to place food into your mouth? Why do most Americans eat three major meals a day, while in other parts of the world, two and sometimes only one is the norm? Why is the majority of food that is consumed in America cooked? Why do many people not consider a meal complete without a sugar dessert?

I don't think it is necessary to ask any more questions because the answer will probably be the same to them all: "That's just the way I was brought up." Thus, we see that tradition has played a great part in determining what we put into our body and the manner in which it is consumed.

Eating Habits Handed Down

Most Christians, like myself, were brought up to eat like their parents before them. I am not saying that our parents meant us any harm; it's just that eating habits tend to be handed down from one generation to the next.

For instance, when I was pastoring a church in eastern North Carolina some years ago, I noticed that people in that area consumed pork in large quantities. In fact, most meals contained two, and sometimes three, different meats, and almost every vegetable dish was prepared with a large piece of "fatback" (the traditional way of eating in that area). Because of those traditional eating habits, there was an extremely high rate of circulatory problems and early deaths caused by clogged arteries.

Tradition plays an extremely large part in the way we eat, what we eat, and the physical problems that we experience.

My Mom Dies After Bout With Cancer

My mother died after a horrible experience with colon cancer. At the age of 42, I was told that I had cancer of the colon. Did this mean that I had an inherent weakness that was passed on to me by my mother (which is strongly taught by many medical authorities)? Or could it be that the way my mom and I ate, and the things we ate, and the way that we lived were similar enough to produce similar physical problems?

My Dad Dies From Heart Attack

My dad had numerous heart attacks and strokes, starting at the age of 42, finally dying from one of these heart attacks. When I was 42 years old, the doctor told me that my body was ripe for a heart attack or stroke. Had I inherited a weak heart and circulatory system from my dad? Or could it be that Dad and I both had eaten a similar diet, prepared in a similar manner along with a similar lifestyle?

How I Responded to Personal Physical Problems

How was I to respond to these physical problems that I was experiencing in my own body? I could have said, "Well, it must be God's will for my life," and just done nothing. Or I could have placed myself in the hands of medical doctors who were unable to help either Mother or Dad. Or thirdly, I could set out on a quest for knowledge, to find out why my body was experiencing these problems, and seek to find a solution. As I stated in Chapter 1, I chose the third option and ultimately changed my diet and lifestyle, and started doing vigorous exercising, along with some other changes.

How My Body Responded

How did my body respond to these changes? Well, let's see how my heart and circulatory system reacted. In 1976, at the age of 42, my blood pressure was normally around 150/90, which is considered borderline high blood pressure. Six years later, at the age of 48, after changing my diet and becoming physically active, my blood pressure was down to 125/75. Then, at age 63, more than 21 years after I was told that my body was ripe for a heart attack or stroke, my blood pressure runs around 110/70.

At age 42, my pulse rate at rest was in the lower 70s. Later, at the age of 63, my pulse rate at rest was in the upper 40s. Even after jogging five miles in less than an hour, my pulse rate is under 120.

Now I ask you a question: "Would you say that my physical problems at the age of 42 were (a) the will of God, (b) weaknesses inherited from my parents, or (c) the results of tradition? Or possibly the result of a combination of two causes: tradition and altered tradition?

Altered Tradition

The traditional eating habits of most Americans have been altered by the strong advertising of today's food merchants, the fast-food craze, and a faster pace of life. Let's explore altered tradition with another personal illustration.

My mother's parents, my grandparents, were both hard-working farm people...out in the fields at the crack of dawn, living a simple life of hard work and eating primarily simple meals prepared from the food raised in their own gardens and orchard. They didn't even have electricity or running water. Yet, both remained strong and active into their 80s.

From this strong stock, their daughter, my mother, was in serious physical trouble before the age of 50. Then her son (yours truly) was in serious physical trouble by the age of 42. You can clearly see the downward progression of health from one generation to the next.

Does altered tradition have anything to do with why Christians get sick? (When I talk about altered tradition, I'm talking about a change from the way our ancestors grew, processed, prepared, and consumed their food in comparison to today.) Let's explore this thought.

Chemicals

For instance, prior to World War II there was very little use of insecticides (chemical poisons) used in the growing of food. Today, over 1,000,000,000 (one billion) pounds of insecticides are sprayed or dusted on the food Americans consume each year. Incidentally, less than 1% of that billion pounds of insecticides ever reaches the insects it was intended to destroy.

In the early days of insecticides, you could at least wash off the poison or remove the poison by peeling the fruit or vegetable. Today there are systemic poisons that are taken in by the plant and become an integral part of the plant. Thus the poison is on the inside and impossible to remove.

I've just talked about the insecticides. In the raising of our food today, herbicides (poisons) are used to kill weeds, and fungicides to destroy fungi or inhibit their growth. Unless you have your own garden or have access to produce raised on an organic farm, it is impossible to escape these poisons.

"Pesticides can damage and tax your immune system at the same time. The damage can be both acute and cumulative. Since many toxic chemicals are stored in your fat cells and lymph glands, they can remain in the body for decades. Thus, health problems can build up over a long period in ways that science doesn't yet fully understand. One of the most dangerous effects of pesticides is that they weaken your immune system so you are less able to combat even ordinary infections. Symptoms of a weakened immune system might include: skin rashes, nausea, fatigue, depression, leukemia, frequent infections and fever" (*Organic Gardening* magazine, April 1988, p. 59).

Preservatives

When our grandparents were growing up, the only preservatives used in food were salt and vinegar. Today, with modern processing, it is hard to find a prepared food that doesn't contain chemical preservatives, along with artificial colorings, artificial flavorings, stabilizers, emulsifiers, and so forth.

Most of the additives that have been tested have been proven to cause harmful effects on the test animals—yet the average American consumes over seven pounds of these poisons annually. There are literally thousands of different toxic chemicals being used on our foods today: BHA, BHT, sodium nitrate, sodium nitrite, calcium propionate, EDTA, red dyes, yellow dyes, and the list goes on and on and on. Let's look at just one example:

Beatrice Hunter, in her book *Food Additives and Your Health*, states on pages 47-48 that "severe allergic reactions have been reported for BHT (and BHA), including 'debilitating and disabling chronic asthmatic attacks, skin blistering, eye hemorrhaging, tingling sensations on face and hands, extreme weakness, fatigue, edema, chest tightness and difficulty in breathing.'"

There is no such thing as a *safe* chemical! All chemicals are toxic to the body and produce adverse reactions within the body!

Most Americans just take it for granted that if a product is sold for food then it is safe to eat. Not so! It's also amazing, but true, that the average person never associates his physical problems with what he eats or drinks.

Water

Our ancestors drank water from a well or spring that was basically pure. The water most people drink today comes from a municipal water supply that has been chlorinated, fluoridated, and usually contains a host of impurities and toxic materials.

Even most wells and springs have been contaminated by the pollution of our ground water from chemical poisons used in farming and from chemical spills and dumps. We'll talk more about water in later chapters.

Milk

Milk is another example. As a child, I often visited my aunt and uncle's farm. After the morning milking, some of the fresh, warm milk was placed in a pitcher on the breakfast table within minutes after leaving the cow. This fresh milk received no processing.

Today milk goes from the cow to bulk holding tanks for cooling. Then it is picked up by a tanker truck that hauls it to a processing plant. At the processing plant it is pasteurized—heated to at least 160 degrees to kill bacteria (the heating also destroys almost the total nutritional value of the milk). Then it is homogenized so that the cream won't rise to the top, and finally coal-tar-derived vitamins are added in an attempt to replace some of the natural vitamins removed in processing. After processing, it is placed in plastic, waxed cardboard, or, on occasion, glass containers and ultimately finds its way into the home and the body.

We are told that milk is a great source of calcium. Yet most people are unaware that pasteurization (the heating process) renders the calcium unusable by the body. The reason? Heat changes the organic calcium found in raw milk to an inorganic form. The body can only utilize organic minerals.

As a boy, I can remember having a terrible problem with cavities in my teeth. The dentist told my parents to increase the amount of milk I drank. My parents did just that. I consumed large quantities of pasteurized milk. But instead of the number of cavities being reduced, the number of cavities increased!

Flour

What have the processors done with whole wheat flour? Well, the first thing that they do is remove the germ, which contains most of the food value, because it gums up their machinery. Next, they remove the bran because it leaves brown specks in the flour.

By the way, both the wheat germ and the wheat bran are then sold back to the public in health food stores as health foods.

They then take what is left after removing the germ and bran and bleach it, with chemical bleaching agents similar to Clorox, to make it nice and white. Next, they add coal-tar-derived vitamins, package it, and sell it to the unsuspecting public as enriched flour.

That's sure a far cry from the way our ancestors made their flour. And can you imagine the nutritional value in today's baked products? Try reading the label on the next loaf of bread you buy.

Oils and Fats

Other items that have been altered are oils and fats. In past generations, butter and lard were the leading oils and fats used in America. Butter was made from unpasteurized raw milk and usually no salt was added. Most people today realize that lard was and is a very harmful substance to the body.

Modern technology and processing has brought us a substitute for butter that is usually less costly and is often promoted as being better for you than butter—it is called margarine. Margarine is made by taking liquid oil, heating it to a high temperature, and then bubbling hydrogen gas through it until it becomes hardened. Then it is bleached, filtered, and deodorized, producing an odorless, tasteless, artificial fat!

This process changes a polyunsaturated oil into a ***totally saturated fat***—the kind that causes high cholesterol problems and clogs the arteries, which ultimately results in heart attacks, strokes, and cancer. The ultimate product is a substance very similar to lard, a substance the body has no means of digesting.

Besides being used in margarine, hydrogenated oils and fat are used extensively in shortening, baked and fried products, and most brands of peanut butter. Some nutritionists believe that margarine is the single most *dangerous* "so-called" food on the American market!

Meat

Are animals (from which we get our meat) being raised today any differently from the way they were in our grandparents' day? The answer to that question is "yes"! All sorts of drugs are being added to the animals' food and drink, like antibiotics to keep them well and growth hormones to cause them to grow faster.

Chickens that lay eggs sold in the market usually never see the light of day. These animals are raised in wire cages where they can hardly move, so that all energy will go into egg production. Their food and water is brought to them automatically by conveyor. Various chemical substances, including antibiotics, are added to feed and water.

This is certainly far removed from the backyard flocks our ancestors kept, which were able to eat greens, bugs, and worms, as well as having sunlight and a rooster, each adding nutrition to the egg.

We could go on with many other illustrations, but I believe it is clear to any thinking person that there is hardly a single food in the marketplace today that hasn't been altered in some way from the way it was raised or prepared in past generations.

Fast Foods

We are living in a day where the pace of life is too fast. People are too busy to prepare meals in the traditional way. Fast-food restaurants are on every corner. Microwave ovens and convenience foods are the norm.

Most people today feel that these convenience foods are a blessing, in that they require less time for preparation. But are they a blessing or are they helping to contribute to the multitude of physical problems plaguing the families of today?

I'll just give one example, which will hopefully help you to understand the hazard in convenience foods. All canned, bottled, and most frozen fruit juices are heated to high temperatures so that they have an extended shelf life without spoilage. Someone reading the preceding sentence might possibly say, "So what if these juices are heated with high heat? What's the big deal about that?"

To show why it is a "big deal" if you want to be physically strong and healthy, we will look more closely at just one juice: orange juice.

Orange Juice

In order to make frozen orange juice into concentrate, they first squeeze the juice from the orange. Next, the moisture content is removed either by boiling it away or by spray drying. Both methods use high heat to remove this moisture and produce an orange juice concentrate.

The concentrate is then frozen and placed in storage until shipped to the wholesaler and finally to the retailer. The consumer then purchases this frozen concentrate and reconstitutes it by replacing the liquid that had previously been removed from it. The water added is usually from a municipal water supply.

Here is the problem: When the orange juice was subjected to the high temperatures, it lost 100% of its enzymes, over 80% of the vitamins, and 100% of the organic minerals that were in the fresh juice. In other words, the processing destroyed almost the entire nutritional value of the original freshly squeezed juice. Also, the water added in reconstituting the juice was inferior to the liquid removed originally.

Today we have been programmed to accept ease, speed, and convenience, little realizing that each step of processing takes us further from the real thing!

Vitamins

"Vitamins?" most of our ancestors would ask. "What are they?" The food merchants remove most of the nutrients in order to keep foods from spoiling, as we saw above. Then they often add various substances so that the food will taste better, look nicer, and smell good. Finally, they add preservatives so that the product will have a longer shelf life, which increases sales and profits.

Then, after the nutrients are all but totally destroyed in processing, the food industry adds vitamins that will supposedly make up for the nutritional loss. Don't believe it! It just doesn't work that way! They cannot replace the nutrients that were originally in the whole living food with something dead and artificial.

Gasoline

As I mentioned earlier in the book, it is probably not an exaggeration to say that most Christians are more concerned with the brand and grade of gasoline they put into their automobiles than they are about the quality and nutritional value of the food they put into their bodies.

This was true in my own life. Not that I was intentionally trying to destroy myself, or that I didn't care about my body, I was just lacking in knowledge! I was really very ignorant concerning this subject. I was the victim of tradition and altered tradition. I contend that much of the sickness and physical problems among Christians today can be traced directly to this cause.

In the Bible, in Genesis 6:12, we see where God destroyed most of His creation because man *"had corrupted God's way upon the earth."* Man had changed things from the way God intended them to be.

As far as the food we eat, we most certainly have changed it from the way our Creator made it and intended it to be. We poison it while it is growing, remove the nutrients in processing, add toxic substances to it, and then blame God when we get sick. May God help us!

Chapter 4—In Review

1. Christians are often lacking in knowledge concerning the relationship between food, nutrition, lifestyle, and health.

2. Many of our physical problems stem from following the traditional methods of preparing and eating our foods.

3. Altered tradition has most certainly played its part by changing the food from the manner in which God intended it to be consumed.

4. Poisons are added to our food while it is being grown.

5. Poisons are added to our foods during processing.

6. Poisons are added to our drinking water.

7. Most of the nutrients in milk are destroyed during processing.

8. During processing, flour not only has the nutrients removed, but then it is bleached and has artificial nutrients added.

9. Some nutritionists believe that margarine is the single most dangerous food on the American market.

10. Meat and eggs are tampered with.

11. Fast foods and convenience foods are usually far removed from the real thing.

12. Almost 6,000 years ago, God destroyed most of His creation because man had changed things from the way He intended them to be.

CHAPTER 5

DRUGS AND THE

MEDICAL PROFESSION

———————

And a certain woman, which had an issue of blood twelve years, and had suffered many things of many physicians, and had spent all that she had, and was nothing bettered but rather grew worse (Mark 5:25-26).

D
an Rather, in a TV broadcast *CBS Reports* on January 10, 1975, said:

"During 1974, Senate hearings, under the chairmanship of Senator Edward Kennedy, focused on problems of drug use and safety. Senator Kennedy said, 'This is a serious public health issue, and it's one that is generally not understood among the American people...and one that results in the death of, as we've heard estimated, anywhere from 40,000 to 120,000 deaths a year. We can't be specifically sure of the number. Some have said that it's a good deal higher. We've had estimates before our committee

from responsible researchers that say the American consumer is paying $2,000,000,000 (two billion dollars) a year
more than he should because of adverse drug reactions.'"

My Christian friend, that was disclosed in 1974! Since then,
the problem has grown much worse. And remember, we're talking
about so-called *legal* drugs, prescribed by the medical profession.

The Medicine Man

In some parts of the world, people still believe disease and
sickness is the work of an evil spirit. So when they become sick,
they summon the "medicine man" or "witch doctor" who comes
and prepares a vile concoction for them, which they then pour
down their throats in hopes of getting well. We think of that as
being very crude and primitive, but, really now, have we advanced
much further in this so-called "enlightened" generation?

Today when someone gets sick, he goes to a man or woman
called a "medical doctor." This medical doctor asks him what the
problem is, often gives him some kind of an examination, and
then, in language the person can't understand, writes something
on a piece of paper (called a prescription). The sick person then
takes that piece of paper to a drugstore where the druggist takes
that piece of paper, mixes the potion prescribed (or reaches for the
drug already mixed), puts it into a bottle, and the sick person pays
the price. The sick person then takes this unknown substance
(drug) into his body, hoping it will bring relief from the symptoms.
Talk about faith!

If the medical doctor can't find the drug that will relieve the
symptoms, he sends the sick person home and classifies him as
incurable or may suggest that the problem is psychological. Have
we really come as far as we think from the days of the "medicine
man" and "witch doctor"?

We Live in a Drug-Oriented Society

We live in a drug-oriented society! Our water is drugged with
chlorine and fluoride (sodium fluoride). Chlorine is a bleaching

agent. Sodium fluoride is used as a roach and rat poison. If there is enough chlorine in the water you drink that you can smell it, there is enough chlorine to destroy the friendly bacteria in your intestinal tract and thus deprive your body of important vitamins that these friendly bacteria manufacture for us, including vitamin B12.

Our foods have been drugged with some 7,000 different chemicals (drugs): sodium nitrate, sodium nitrite, BHA, BHT, EDTA, and a host of other preservatives (drugs), artificial flavorings (drugs), and colorings (drugs). About 1,000,000,000 (one billion) pounds of these drugs per year are consumed in America—that is over seven pounds for every man, woman, and child every year!

Then, when we get sick from the drugs in our drinking water and from taking devitalized, drugged, so-called food substances into our body, we call the medical doctor. The medical doctor, a doctor licensed to practice the prescribing of drugs, writes a prescription for some more drugs, which is taken to the pharmacist ("one engaged in preparing, preserving, compounding, and dispensing drugs," says Webster). The pharmacist dispenses and sells the drugs. The sick person, whose sickness may quite possibly be a drug reaction from drugged water and food, then takes these additional drugs, supposedly to cure his illness. How pathetic... and we think we are so knowledgeable!

Aspirin

Every year, Americans consume over 16,000,000,000 (16 billion) aspirin. A drug that kills many persons legally each year! This is a nonprescription drug that has never cured anyone!

However, it does cover up God's natural warning signal. For example, a headache is a warning signal, warning of an internal problem. How does the average American react to this warning signal? Why, he takes an aspirin or two, or three, and sometimes even more. What effect do these aspirin have on the body? They drug the body, thus relieving the pain, and short-circuit the body's warning device.

How should we respond when we get a headache or suffer from some other form of illness? Find the cause, eliminate the cause, and thus the headache or whatever the illness may be, will go away. And it will stay away as long as we stay away from what caused the headache or illness in the first place!

Christians Are Drug-Oriented

It is sad, but true, that Christians are just as drug-oriented as non-Christians. If Christians have a headache, they take a drug; if they can't sleep, they take a drug; if pregnancy is not desired, they take a drug; if nervous, they take a drug. Drugs are even used to slow down an overactive child when the overactive child's problem is usually caused by the drug he has been consuming in his food or drink.

Christians have been deceived into taking drugs because they are so widely used, advertised, and are such an important part of the society in which we live. Often, Christians try to differentiate between "good" drugs and "bad" drugs...probably because they do not understand what drugs are, what effect they have on the body, and what the Bible has to say about them!

What Is a Drug?

Webster's dictionary defines a drug as "a substance other than food intended to affect the structure or function of the body."

As Christians, we need to realize that God is constantly warning against the use of all drugs and the deception of drugs. The biblical word for *sorceries* comes from the Greek word *phar-ma-kia*, which today in the English language we call drugs. Revelation 18:23 says, "*...for by thy sorceries* [drugs] *were all nations deceived.*"

Today, most Christians have been deceived concerning drugs. They stand strongly and boldly against heroin, cocaine, crack, marijuana, and the like. Also, most Christians will not allow the drug of alcohol—from beer, wine, or whiskey—to enter their bodies. Most Christians refrain from the use of tobacco, and the drug, nicotine, isn't allowed to enter the body by way of smoking or chewing.

Why do Christians stand against these drugs? Because "these drugs are harmful and against God's will," we tell ourselves and our children. We also teach against them from the pulpits of our churches.

And yet Christians indulge in the taking of aspirin, sleeping pills, nerve pills, etc., and readily accept every pill and prescription the medical doctor prescribes without hesitation. My Christian friend, these are also drugs and often just as harmful and contrary to the Word of God as is the cocaine, alcohol, and nicotine that we condemn!

All Drugs Are Foreign Substances and Poisons to the Body

All drugs are toxic and have a poisoning effect on the body! God made a fantastic body and He never intended for these foreign substances (drugs) to enter it. But when they do enter the body, the body mobilizes its forces in an all-out effort to remove these foreign, poisonous substances through every avenue at its disposal.

The Common Cold

Take, for example, the common cold for which the medical profession has spent billions of taxpayers' dollars trying to find the cause and cure, but never has and never will! Why? Because they are looking for a germ or virus...and that is the wrong place to look.

A cold is nothing more than the all-wise, God-created body making an effort to cleanse itself of an accumulation of toxic waste!

What has the medical establishment told us to do? Stop the cold symptoms. "Take some aspirin (drug) to take away the headache and possible fever." "Take a decongestant or antihistamine (drugs) to stop the nose from running." Thus, the body is drugged. The headache, a warning signal, goes away. The runny nose, which was removing copious amounts of poisons from the body, dries up. The person says, "Praise the Lord, my cold is gone!"

But what that person doesn't realize is that the poisons that were trying to make their way out of the body *are still in the body* and will try again. The next time, it might be another cold, or it might be something more serious, like cancer.

Most Christians would not deliberately or knowingly try to poison their own bodies. But when that poison (drug) is called *medicine* they readily accept it as something that is all right to put into the body, no matter how vile it tastes or how violently the body reacts against it. Only children seem to have enough sense to reject it. They often have to be forced into taking medicine or have it sugar-coated (another drug) to make it palatable.

The Results

What has been the result of the mass drugging of the American population, including Christians? *Rodale Press* has published figures to show that at least 200,000 Americans die annually at the hands of doctors! Another newspaper states that 4,500,000 people each year are poisoned (drugged) so seriously by their physicians that they require hospitalization!

Over 40,000 die of this form of doctoring each year, and many believe this number exceeds 120,000, according to the Dan Rather report at the beginning of this chapter. Remember, all drugs or medicines are inherently poisonous, and side effects or adverse reactions are just another way of saying poisonous effects or reactions!

We Cannot Be Drugged Into Health

People cannot be drugged (poisoned) into health! Drugs create problems rather than solve them. To regain health, the sick person must cleanse the body of the drugs and toxic substances that have accumulated and then provide the body with the proper building materials and influences that will allow the body to purify, repair, and rebuild itself.

Health *cannot* be restored by taking drugs! Drugs cannot rebuild the cells of the body! The body is self-healing when healthful practices are followed. Just as you are able to witness the healing of a cut, covered by a scab, followed by new skin on the exterior as the body heals itself, just so, it heals on the inside when conditions are made favorable for it to do so!

A Doctor Speaks

Sir William A. Lane, a world authority on medical matters and long regarded as England's foremost abdominal surgeon, when entertained by the staff of Johns Hopkins Hospital and Medical College, said:

> "Gentlemen, I will never die of cancer! I am taking measures to prevent it. It is caused by poisons created in our bodies by the food we eat. What we should do then, if we would avoid cancer, is to eat raw fruits and vegetables. First, that we may be better nourished; secondly, that we may more easily eliminate waste products. We have been studying germs when we should have been studying diet and drainage. The world has been on the wrong track. The answer has been within ourselves all the time; drain the body of its poisons, feed it properly, and the miracle is done. Nobody need have cancer who will take the trouble to avoid it."

Thank you, Dr. Lane!

Chapter 5—In Review

1. We live in a drug-oriented society; even our water and food are drugged!

2. We take drugs to cure the physical problems often brought on by the taking of devitalized, processed, and drugged substances into our bodies.

3. A drug, says Webster's dictionary, is a "substance other than food intended to affect the structure or function of the body."

4. The Bible warns us against the use of all drugs and the deception of drugs.

5. All drugs are poisons to our bodies.

6. We cannot be drugged or poisoned into health!

7. Health comes only when the body is provided with the proper materials to cleanse the poisons from the systems and rebuild new, living, strong, vital, vibrant cells.

8. God made a body that is self-healing and will heal itself when given the opportunity!

CHAPTER 6

OTHER DRUGS

———❦———

...for by thy sorceries [drugs] *were all nations deceived* (Revelation 18:23).

In this chapter we will continue our review of drugs as a cause of sickness. Only these drugs are all legal, readily available without prescription, and most of them are consumed by Christians on a regular basis.

As we start our examination of these legal, non-medical drugs, let's remember that a drug is: "a substance other than food intended to affect the structure or function of the body" (Webster's dictionary).

All of the drugs in this chapter are non-food substances, although most readers of this book will not recognize some of them as drugs. Nor are these drugs normally taken with the intention of affecting the function or structure of the body. Nonetheless, by intent or not, or with knowledge or not, they *all affect* the structure and/or function of the body.

We will begin with those that most Christians will readily recognize as drugs and then talk about some drugs that may surprise the average reader…because they are not often recognized as drugs by most Christians.

Alcohol

"Wine is a mocker, strong drink is raging: and whosoever is deceived thereby is not wise" (Prov. 20:1). *"At the last it biteth like a serpent, and stingeth like an adder"* (Prov. 23:32).

Most Christians recognize alcohol as a drug that destroys, maims, and kills. Just on the highways of our nation, some 25,000 people are killed by alcohol each year, while tens of thousands are maimed for the rest of their lives. Then there are the multitudes of broken homes and divorces, along with the abused spouses and children.

Yet this addictive narcotic drug is a "legal beverage" in most cities and towns in our great nation. There is abundant documentation of alcohol's destructive effect on society. But let's delve into another aspect of beverage alcohol and see what it does to the body of the person who consumes it.

Alcohol—A Deadly Poisonous Drug

In the process of making beverage alcohol, they begin with a natural, non-drug liquid. If taken into the body in its natural state, this liquid would have a beneficial reaction on the cells of the body (example: grape juice). However, in changing it from a natural state into alcohol, it has to go through a process called fermentation, a process of bacterial action that causes the natural liquid to break down and decay.

The end product of fermentation is alcohol. It can be purchased as beer, wine, or liquor. What most people do not realize, however, is that alcohol—no matter what form it is in or what it is called or how legal it may be to purchase—is a deadly poisonous drug.

How Alcohol Affects the Body

When alcohol is taken into the body, it not only temporarily affects the functioning of the brain, causing people to do all kinds of crazy things under its influence, but it does irreparable damage to the cells, membranes, and tissues as it travels through the body. In fact, it literally destroys body cells while raising havoc with the liver.

If a person continues to use alcohol over a period of time, the liver cells start to die in increasing numbers and these living cells are replaced with scar tissue. As the use of alcohol continues, the liver enlarges, and then, in the advanced stages of its demise, the liver starts to shrivel and is unable to function. Once the liver reaches this state, an irreversible point has been reached and death is not far off!

So we see that consuming alcohol is not only unbiblical—it's a narcotic drug that causes people to do crazy things and is a killer on the highways and a leading cause of broken homes, abuse, and divorce—but the user of this drug is slowly committing suicide, as the alcohol literally destroys the cells of his body.

Tobacco

Many religious groups and churches teach and preach against the use of tobacco. Yet it is a known fact that many Christians use tobacco. For abundant proof of this, stand outside the front door or check the parking lot of almost any church, following a church service, and see just how many parishioners can't wait to "light up"! Why the rush and urgency to light up? These people are addicted to the narcotic drug called *nicotine*. They are literally drug addicts and their bodies are screaming for a "fix"!

The Smoking Slipper

Some Christians try to hide their use of tobacco. I will never forget an incident while I was pastoring a country church some years ago.

In this church there was a deacon I had inherited when I became pastor. He smoked cigars but was always careful not to smoke while I was around, though his clothes reeked from the cigar smoke, always a dead giveaway.

One day I heard that he was at home sick, so I went to visit him. After knocking on the door, a voice inside said, "Come in." Obviously he did not realize it was the preacher because as I entered the room there was a big cigar in his hand. When he realized who his visitor was, he quickly threw the cigar into his slipper. As the smoke billowed out of that slipper, I made my visit very short lest his slipper go up in smoke also, and he be further embarrassed!

I have often thought of that incident with a chuckle, but it is also very sad. To see people become slaves to the drug nicotine is bad enough, but when you realize what that drug is doing to their body, it becomes a tragedy.

How Nicotine Affects the User

Nicotine is one of the most lethal poisons Americans take into their bodies on a regular basis. It is just as much a narcotic drug as cocaine, marijuana, heroin, opium, or morphine. Tobacco smoke contains over 16 different poisons—tars and oxidation products.

God gave us lungs as a means of taking into our bodies clean, pure, fresh air. From the air, the body receives its primary nutritional need: oxygen. The lungs take in this oxygen and it is sent throughout the body to nourish the cells.

When a person smokes, the lungs become coated and clogged with tars and other poisons from the smoke, thus causing a malfunction of the lungs. As a result, the body becomes unable to take in sufficient oxygen to meet its needs and starvation, malnutrition, and enervation of the body results. As the same time, toxins are accumulating in the body because the lungs cannot properly expel them.

Did you ever notice how smokers do not have the wind or stamina to exert themselves physically for any length of time? This is because the lungs cannot take in sufficient oxygen to supply the body's needs.

As the smoker continues this destructive habit, the effects start to manifest themselves in more serious ways. Shortness of breath is often followed by "smoker's hack," often followed by emphysema, or as I have heard some call it, "an asthma attack." Large numbers of smokers ultimately end up with lung cancer or some other form of cancer, circulation problems, heart trouble, and an early, horrible, often choking death. Every 17 seconds, there is a smoking-related death.

How Smoking Affects Others

If smokers were the only ones harmed by the smoke from a cigarette, cigar, or pipe, it would be tragic enough, but when others are forced to breathe their smoke, it is a double tragedy. Smoking in public places where others are forced to breathe secondhand smoke is a crime against humanity.

And pity the poor child with a smoking parent or a spouse with a smoking partner. There are ample statistics to show that secondhand smoke is just as harmful to the body of the non-smoker as the "firsthand" smoke is to the smoker himself. Also, statistics show a tremendous increase in respiratory problems of children brought up in a smoker's home.

Most drug addictions result in the destruction of only the addict. Smoking, however, not only harms the addict, but his family, friends, and even total strangers.

A Few Words for Smoking Christians

If you are reading this book and are a smoking Christian, why not quit? For the sake of yourself, your family, and the Lord who says, *"What? Know ye not that your body is the temple of the Holy Ghost which is in you, which you have of God, and ye are not your own? For ye are bought with a price: Therefore glorify God in your body, and in your spirit which are God's"* (1 Cor. 6:19-20). Can you in all honesty say smoking glorifies God?

Coffee

If America has a national drink it would have to be coffee. Americans drink coffee with breakfast and sometimes *for* breakfast. Then in mid-morning they have their "coffee break." It's coffee with lunch, again in mid-afternoon, with supper, etc. Over 2,000,000,000 (two billion) pounds of coffee are consumed by Americans each year.

Coffee-drinking seems so innocent and harmless and I can almost hear some reader asking, "There isn't something wrong with coffee, is there? Does coffee harm the body? Is coffee a drug?"

Coffee Is Indeed a Drug

Coffee is not a food. There is nothing in coffee that the body can use, nothing that will build new cells. The only effect coffee has on the body is to tear it down and destroy the cells.

Coffee is a drug! Coffee contains caffeine, along with harmful oils and other toxic substances.

How Coffee Affects the Body

Caffeine is a stimulant! It is called a stimulant because it excites the nerve centers into unusual and injurious activity as the body rallies its forces to expel this poison. At first, caffeine gives a sensation of exhilaration, but its effects are mental depression, nerve exhaustion, decreased muscular power, and damage to the liver and kidneys.

When caffeine first enters the body, the blood pressure increases and the heart beats more forcefully, but as the drug is expelled from the body, the body beats with less force and the blood pressure falls below normal.

Caffeine causes the kidneys to work overtime in an effort to expel this poison, but as coffee drinking continues, the kidneys are weakened and become less efficient. Degeneration of the kidneys is the end result.

The volatile oils in coffee irritate the lining of the stomach and the intestines, causing frequency of urination. This irritation can lead to ulcers, gastritis, spontaneous abortions, still births, premature births, and a host of other problems.

Because the poisoning effects of caffeine on the body are so slow, most coffee drinkers do not realize that their habit is slowly destroying parts of their body.

Remember coffee is not a food, but a poisonous, addictive drug that can only do great harm to the body while it is incapable of doing it any good.

Tea

The drug in tea is called *theine*. A check of Webster's dictionary will reveal that theine is just another word for caffeine. Tea contains about one-half the amount of caffeine as does coffee, but still has the same poisoning effects on the body. It just poisons the consumer a little more slowly and takes a little longer to destroy body parts.

Colas and Soft Drinks

This may come as a surprise, but all cola drinks and most soft drinks contain caffeine! And caffeine is an addictive drug. By putting caffeine in colas and soft drinks, a literal addiction is created, which has made the soft-drink industry one of the wealthiest industries in the nation. Many children begin their addiction for this drug through the soda bottle!

Webster's dictionary says that *cola* is a "carbonated soft drink flavored with extract from coca leaves, kola nut, sugar, caramel, and acid and aromatic substances." A further check of Webster's dictionary reveals that cocaine is "a bitter crystalline alkaloid...obtained from coca leaves." Regarding the kola nut, Webster says, "the bitter caffeine-containing seed of a kola tree used...in beverages."

Those who drink colas and soft drinks containing caffeine will subject themselves to the same problems by caffeine as we saw under the heading "Coffee." Soft drinks are especially destructive to children, often causing them to experience irritability, irregular heartbeat, insomnia, and hyperactivity, just to name a few.

Chocolate

It may come as a surprise to the reader that chocolate, which is derived from the ground, roasted seeds of the cocoa tree, is an addictive drug! Cocoa or chocolate contains the drug theobromine. Random House dictionary defines *theobromine* as "a poisonous powder, used chiefly as a diuretic, myocardial stimulant… found in cocoa." Webster's dictionary says that theobromine is "a bitter alkaloid…closely related to caffeine…and has stimulant properties."

Chocolate and cocoa are stimulants because when they are taken into the body, the body immediately mobilizes its forces to rid itself of this poisonous drug as quickly as possible. Pimples are just one of the avenues the body uses to try to rid itself of this poisonous drug. And as Webster said, theobromine is a form of caffeine and wreaks all of the havoc in the body we learned about under the coffee heading.

Isn't it interesting, and pathetic, how many harmful substances we take into our bodies because sugar has been added by the food industry to trick or fool our taste buds into letting them enter? And speaking of sugar…

Sugar

Glucose, fructose, and sucrose are naturally occurring sugars found in raw fruits, vegetables, and honey. Glucose is a simple sugar that is released quickly into the bloodstream. Fructose is slowly converted to glucose. Sucrose is made of equal amounts of glucose and fructose. To be utilized it, too, is converted into glucose. Glucose is the form of sugar that our bodies most readily use.

Glucose is very easily and readily assimilated by the body and is a very basic and necessary food, providing fuel for the cells of the body. Webster's dictionary says of glucose that it is the "form that occurs widely in nature and is the usual form in which carbohydrate is assimilated by animals."

Honey is mostly glucose and fructose, while maple syrup and dates provide mostly sucrose.

High concentrations of sucrose are naturally found in sugar beets and sugar cane. The refiners use some 14 steps in processing the natural product, in the refining of sucrose. During this processing, the refiners remove the B-complex, enzymes, proteins, minerals, and vitamins. This processing produces a devitalized chemical substance containing no vitamins, minerals, or God-given phytonutrients. It is just pure carbohydrate! And it is capable of doing tremendous harm to the body.

Most Processed Foods Contain Sucrose

A careful reading of the ingredient labels on food products found on the supermarket shelves, would reveal sugar or salt or both, in almost every manufactured product. Without sugar and/or salt, the food manufacturers would not be able to sell their products; our taste buds would reject these dead, devitalized, toxic, so-called "food" products. You will even find sugar or salt in such products as toothpaste, mouthwash, tobacco, chewing gum, etc.

Sugar Is Addictive

The average American begins his addiction to sugar shortly after birth when a nurse puts a bottle of sugar water into the infant's mouth. This is followed by adding sugar to the infant's formula so the baby will drink this unnatural substance. The commercial baby food industry puts sugar into their processed food products so the babies' taste buds will not reject these unnatural products.

Then there are the breakfast cereals, many of which contain in excess of 50% sugar. Ice cream usually contains about 33% sugar. A

12-ounce can or bottle of cola or soft drink contains about 8-11 teaspoons of sugar, and that is just the beginning of an endless list.

At the turn of the century, the annual consumption of sugar in the form of sucrose was approximately seven pounds for every person in the United States. By 1964, this figure had jumped to around 95 pounds. Today the average intake of sucrose by every man, woman, and child in our country is in excess of 125 pounds! We have literally become a nation of sugar addicts.

At creation, God placed in man a natural desire for sugar. However, the commercial food industry has taken this God-given desire for natural sugar and used it to make tremendous profit from an unsuspecting public. They have substituted concentrated refined sugar for sweet fruits, and thus fooled and perverted man's taste buds.

What Effect Refined Sugar Has on Our Bodies

Refined sugar has a toxic, poisoning, drugging effect on the body. When sugar is consumed in the refined form, it can ferment in the body and cause the formation of carbonic acid, acetic acid, and alcohol.

Acetic acid is very destructive to the cells of the body, literally burning them. It also has a paralyzing effect on the nerves. The alcohol can cause reactions similar in behavior to beverage alcohol, even to the extent of violent actions. The alcohol also has a damaging effect on the kidneys. It affects the nerve and brain function of the body, especially concentration, observation, and locomotion.

As consumption of unnatural sugar continues, the pancreas starts to have problems. The large volume of sucrose causes the pancreas to be tremendously overworked and it begins to malfunction. Many problems can result, probably two of the most serious are hypoglycemia and diabetes.

Most readers are familiar with diabetes, but hypoglycemia creates unbelievable problems as well, and the sad thing is that most of those who suffer from it aren't aware they even have it. Some of the symptoms of hypoglycemia are headaches, irritability, depression, fatigue, inability to concentrate, being upset with spouse or children for no apparent reason, etc. Some marriage counselors familiar with hypoglycemia estimate that upward of 50% of all marriage problems can be traced to this condition!

Sucrose also leaches vitamin B from the body, depletes calcium, shatters the nervous system, causes teeth to decay, hair to fall out, senility, circulation problems, heart trouble, and a host of other problems.

Just drinking one 12-ounce can or bottle of soda a day can add 12 pounds of weight to the body in a year because of its high sugar (sucrose) content. Many studies have shown sucrose to be one of the main causes of discipline problems with children, and often the root cause leading to alcoholism, crime, rape, murder, and a host of other social ills.

Most Christians consume large amounts of sucrose daily. You might find it interesting to check your daily intake. Read the ingredient label of every processed food item that you purchase; the closer the word *sugar* is to the beginning of the listing, the higher the percentage of sugar in that product.

Dr. C. Samuel West, in his book *The Golden Seven Plus One*, states on page 102, "If you fail to do something about your 'simple' sugar intake, beginning today, you will be committing willful suicide!"

Salt

Salt in the form of sodium chloride is a deadly, poisonous, addicting drug and possibly the greatest killer of mankind!

For years, the medical profession told us that it was necessary to take additional salt or salt tablets into our body during hot weather when the body was sweating excessively. They reasoned that the large amounts of salt being excreted from the pores of the body had to be replaced. After causing untold physical suffering for mankind, due to their lack of understanding of how the human body functions, they finally acknowledged that they were wrong. Now the medical profession has reversed itself and says that we should not take extra salt into our bodies, but, rather, eliminate salt from our diet or at least cut down drastically on our consumption.

Earth salt, or even sea salt, is an inorganic form of sodium that cannot be utilized by the body. It enters the body as sodium chloride and what the body can't eliminate through the urine or sweat glands is stored in the tissues of the body as sodium chloride. When it is finally able to exit from the body, it is still sodium chloride. But it has left a trail of woe and destruction all along the way, from entry to exit!

What was really happening when the medical profession found all of that sodium chloride exiting the body through the sweat glands was that the body was using the pores as a means of ridding itself of this deadly poison. God has made a marvelous body, always trying to cleanse the temple of toxic substances and keep itself clean and pure!

How Salt Affects the Body

When salt, in the form of sodium chloride, enters the body, it draws water from the bloodstream, causing the body to send out an SOS signal that manifests itself in thirst. An example would be: After consuming a bowl of soup, which usually contains lots of salt, the body sends a signal to the brain. "Help! Send water!" Why? Because the water helps dilute the salt concentration in order to help neutralize its poisoning of the body.

However, most people consume so much salt, which is found in almost every commercial food product, that the body can't get all the salt out of the system, so it is carried by the blood and deposited throughout the body in the tissue fluids, in an effort to dilute its devastating effects. When a person goes on a fast, he can lose as much as ten pounds or more in just a few days from the excessive body fluid retained in an effort to neutralize the salt.

These salt deposits are found throughout the body and cause unbelievable harm. Some physical problems caused by salt are hardening of the arteries, arthritis, ulcers, distorted vision and even blindness, high blood pressure, tumors, cancer, and a multitude of other degenerative disorders.

Salt is an antibiotic; it kills life! It is used as a preservative because it kills the bacteria (life) in the food to prevent the natural decomposing of that food. In the body, it is just as much a destroyer and killer of cells and life itself!

Salt begins its addictive influence in the life of a little child when his mother, after cooking all of the flavor and nutrition out of the food, adds salt in an effort to make it taste good according to her taste buds. Most store-bought baby foods are also cooked, often with added salt. When this salted, cooked food is first placed into the baby's mouth, it is usually spit back out. So what does the person feeding the baby do? Push it back in. Baby spits it back out again and the parent forces it back into the young child's mouth until it is accepted. And thus the addiction to salt begins! Granted, it was done in ignorance, but how sad!

Does the body have a need for sodium? Yes, but only in trace amounts and that sodium must be in an organic form for the body to be able to utilize it. Organic sodium occurs naturally in most all fruits and vegetables.

God Gave Us a Marvelous Body

As we learn of all the terrible harmful substances we have been putting into our bodies for so many years, the first reaction one often has is, "It's a miracle we are still alive!"

The reason we are still alive, however, is because our wonderful Creator made such a marvelous body that it will take abuse after abuse, always making every effort to cleanse and rebuild itself until it can just take no more abuse. At this point, it starts to manifest the years of abuse and neglect, with the weakest part of the body breaking down first. If the diet and lifestyle is not changed at this point and the abuse is not halted, the breakdown will continue to the next weakest part of the body, etc.

The bodies of some individuals can withstand more abuse than others, possibly because of extensive exercise, which helps flush out toxins, or possibly because of inheriting physically strong ancestral stock. But you can count on all abusers having a payday some day because of an irreversible law which says, "*Be not deceived; God is not mocked: for whatsoever a man soweth* [in ignorance or with knowledge], *that shall he also reap*" (Gal. 6:7).

Fortunately, even after the body starts to break down, the body will usually respond and rebuild the damaged cells when we cooperate with it and stop abusing, start cleansing, and then properly feed our body...God's temple!

Why Christians get sick and are just as sick as non-Christians and why spiritual Christians are just as sick as Christians who are not as spiritual, should already be evident to every reader of this book. Our diet and lifestyles have been the same!

Chapter 6—In Review

1. Just because a drug is "legal" and readily available does not make it good for the body.

2. All drugs affect the structure and function of the body.

3. Consuming alcohol is not only unbiblical—because it is a narcotic drug that causes people to do crazy things and is a destroyer of lives on the highway and a leading cause of divorce—but it basically leads to the committing of slow suicide, as it literally destroys the cells of the body, which is the temple of God.

4. Tobacco, a narcotic drug, contains some 16 different poisons that coat the lungs and keep them from functioning properly and slowly kills the user and those around him.

5. Coffee contains the drug caffeine, which can cause a multitude of physical problems.

6. Tea, cola, soft drinks, and chocolate all contain the drug caffeine, and all are extremely harmful to the body.

7. Sugar, in the form of sucrose, is a drug that is very addictive and creates many of our physical and emotional and even social problems.

8. Salt is a deadly poisonous drug and possibly the greatest killer of mankind.

9. Fortunately, even after the body starts to break down, the body will usually respond and rebuild the damaged cells when we cooperate with it, stop abusing it, start cleansing it, and then properly feed our body, God's temple.

CHAPTER 7

INSUFFICIENT EXERCISE

In the sweat of thy face shalt thou eat bread... (Genesis 3:19).

When God created man, He made him to be physically active. How do we know this to be true?

First—Because God Commands It!

And the Lord God took the man, and put him into the Garden of Eden to dress it ["cultivate it"—Webster] *and keep it* ["take charge of as a caretaker"—Webster] (Genesis 2:15).

Therefore the Lord God sent him forth from the Garden of Eden, to till ["to work by plowing, sowing, and raising crops"—Webster] *the ground from whence he was taken* (Genesis 3:23).

Six days shalt thou labour, and do all thy work (Exodus 20:9).

If any would not work, neither should he eat. For we hear that there are some which walk among you disorderly, working not at all, but are busybodies. Now them that are such we command and exhort by our Lord Jesus Christ, that with quietness

they work, and eat their own bread ["food"—Webster]
(2 Thessalonians 3:10).

Second—By Example

And Noah began to be an husbandman ["one that plows and
cultivates land: farmer"—Webster] (Genesis 9:20).

Third—The Body Cannot Function Properly Without It

When we study the body and how it was made to function, we
learn that the body cannot function properly without daily, vigorous, physical movement.

God Created Man to Be Physically Active

When God made man, He placed him in a *garden* (Gen. 2:15).
In this garden, God provided the food man was to eat (see Gen.
1:29; 2:9,16). However, after the Fall, there were "thorns and this-
tles" (Gen. 3:18), what we would call weeds, that hindered the
growing of man's food. So in order to grow the food man needed
to sustain life, it was necessary for him to remove the weeds. This
required physical exertion!

From the time of Creation, until quite recently, man physically labored for his food on almost a daily basis. Why, it was just a
few hundred years ago that our founding fathers came to the
shores of this great land and carved out clearings, made gardens,
and thus physically labored for their food. Thanksgiving was the
celebration of an abundant harvest.

The Importance of Gardening

All through history, the major pursuit of man has been the
growing of his own food. In fact, the growing of his own food supply was practiced by the majority of people until not too many
years ago. One of the great tragedies of recent generations has
been the leaving of the land by multitudes of people.

If you are 50 years of age or older, it is probable that your parents or at least your grandparents were farmers. I can still see my

grandmother in her 80s out in the garden before the sun was up, hoeing the weeds between the rows of vegetables. I can remember my grandfather guiding a plow that was being pulled by his horse as he broke up the ground for the garden.

They outlived their daughter, my mother, by almost a quarter of a century. My mom, a country girl, married my dad, a city boy, and moved to the city, bought her food, and lived a very physically inactive life.

What I am trying to say is that God made man to be physically active on a daily basis. This physical activity was to be performed in the great out-of-doors in the fresh air.

Leaving the Land Has Had Its Price

As man has gotten away from the way God intended him to live, man's physical body has paid a terrible price. In fact, I dare say that the average American at age 40 couldn't physically keep up with my farmer grandparents when they were 80.

Americans of today may like being able to open a can of food or take a package of frozen food from the freezer or open a box or package or even go to the supermarket and buy fresh (?) produce, but the physical toll they are paying for these conveniences is incalculable. This easy source of food, which does not require exercise, causes physical problems, great physical suffering, and early deaths.

So we now find ourselves in this present day, not only eating processed, packaged food almost totally devoid of nutritional value and loaded with chemicals, but no physical exercise was required to obtain them.

Why the Body Needs Physical Activity

In order for the body to sustain physical life, four basic ingredients are necessary: Air (oxygen), Water, Food, and Exercise.

Food is the least important of these basic needs, as you can usually live at least 40 days without food. Without water you can't live more than 4 days, and without air you can't live more than 4 minutes. However, without motion, the body cells will slowly die!

The reason the body needs physical activity is that the tissue cells of which the body is composed require daily stimulation to maintain their elasticity and pliability. If they are not exercised on a regular basis, they will become weak and sickly and will begin to malfunction. Ultimately, if these cells continue to go without exercise, they will cease to function; and rather than reproducing healthy, vital, vibrant new cells, as God designed them to do, these cells slowly die, and their deposits accumulate and add to the accumulation of toxins and debris in the body.

The Lymph

The soft tissue cells of the body are constantly bathed in a watery fluid called *lymph*. This lymph has several vitally important functions, which are basically feeding and cleansing the cells. But unlike the blood, which has a pump (the heart) to move the blood through the body, the lymph has no pump.

Because it has no pump, the lymph must depend on the motion or exercise of the body. When the body is exercised vigorously on a regular basis, the lymph moves and performs its feeding and cleansing functions as God intended. But when the body is not exercised, the feeding and cleansing of the body by the lymph is hampered, and the toxins and debris begin to accumulate throughout the body. Deposits of debris further restrict the cleansing of the lymph.

As deposits continue to accumulate, the body cells are cut off from their supply of fresh air (oxygen) and are unable to remove the debris (carbon dioxide and other wastes). Also, the cells are prevented from receiving new building supplies. The whole system begins to malfunction, resulting in a multitude of physical problems including cancer and ultimately death!

Tonsils and Appendix

It is interesting to note that swollen tonsils are one of God's warning devices! When the lymph is burdened with too heavy a load of poisons in the system, the tonsils swell. The medical profession says, "Give the sufferer a drug," which will short-circuit the warning signal. If the drugs do not work, "Cut them out." The doctor removed mine when I was a small child.

Interestingly, all four of our children had bad tonsil problems and the doctor gave them drugs for this condition for years. Finally the doctor wanted to remove them from all four. It was at about this time we learned about diet and health, so rather than having them cut out, we changed their diet and all of the tonsil problems ceased!

The appendix has a function similar to the tonsils. It also swells when the lymph system is overburdened with toxic waste. The medical profession treats the appendix in a similar manner as they do tonsils. If there is a problem, cut it out! When God created man, He didn't make any spare or useless parts!

Muscles

Without exercise, the muscles begin to atrophy ("decrease in size or waste away"—Webster). This is clearly evident when you start to use muscles that have not been exercised in a while. But the most important muscle affected by lack of exercise is the heart muscle.

Without exercise, the heart starts to malfunction, arteries clog, and strokes and heart attacks result. Many deaths occur every year when people suddenly put a heavy exertion on an unexercised heart. Shoveling snow would be a good example of this.

The Importance of Exercise

In my many years of studying the body and how nutrition and exercise relate to it, I have found that a person who exercises vigorously on a regular basis and yet eats a poor diet will usually experience fewer physical problems than the person who eats well but does not exercise. The obvious reason: The person who exercises is better able to remove the toxins and debris from the system.

Without daily, vigorous exercise, tissue cells lose their elasticity, lymph cannot move adequately to cleanse and feed body cells, muscles atrophy, the body does not receive a sufficient supply of oxygen, arteries clog, mental faculties slow, and people become forgetful and eventually senile and death finally results.

There are many other problems caused by insufficient exercise, but hopefully we have shown enough to convince the reader that insufficient, daily, vigorous exercise is one of the leading causes as to why Christians get sick.

Chapter 7—In Review

1. God made man to be physically active.

2. Man's primary physical activity was to be received through the labor necessary to grow his own food supply.

3. Until recent years, most people raised their own food supply.

4. Convenience foods and the easy availability of food for purchase has dramatically reduced the amount of exercise the average person receives and has produced correspondingly increased physical problems.

5. To sustain life, four basic ingredients are necessary: Air (oxygen), Water, Food, and Motion or Exercise.

6. Without daily, vigorous exercise, tissue cells lose their elasticity.

7. Without daily, vigorous exercise, lymph cannot move adequately to cleanse and feed body cells.

8. Without daily, vigorous exercise, muscles atrophy ("decrease in size or waste away"—Webster).

9. Insufficient daily, vigorous exercise is one of the leading causes of why Christians get sick.

CHAPTER 8

STRESS AND NEGATIVE EMOTIONS

And the peace of God, which passeth all understanding, shall keep your hearts and minds through Christ Jesus. Finally, brethren, whatsoever things are true, whatsoever things are honest, whatsoever things are just, whatsoever things are pure, whatsoever things are lovely, whatsoever things are of good report; if there be any virtue, and if there be any praise, think on these things...for I have learned, in whatsoever state I am, therewith to be content (Philippians 4:7-8,11).

During my nearly 20 years in the ministry, coming in contact with multitudes of Christians, I found an unusually high percentage of Christians with emotional problems. In fact, there are many ministries that deal exclusively with Christians who have emotional problems.

Now emotional problems are definitely a form of sickness; however, it is a sickness that many do not want to recognize or acknowledge as sickness. In fact, many do not want to acknowledge that they even have a problem. And sadly, when help is finally sought, the help often does not deal with the cause, but rather with the symptoms.

Jesus Wants Us to Be Happy

As we read the Bible, we have to come to the conclusion that the Lord wants us to be happy. *"Blessed is everyone that feareth the Lord; that walketh in His ways…happy shalt thou be, and it shall be well with thee"* (Ps. 128:1-2). *"Happy is that people whose God is the Lord"* (Ps. 144:15). *"Whoso trusteth in the Lord, happy is he"* (Prov. 16:20). Jesus said, *"I am come that they might have life, and that they might have it more abundantly"* (John 10:10).

Are Christians Happy?

But how many Christians do you personally know who are living a really happy, abundant, vibrant Christian life? And if not, why not?

It seems that in many Christian circles, there is a tendency to blame everything on sin. If you are sick, someone will invariably say, "You need to get your heart right with the Lord." Or if unhappy, they might say, "You know, if you were right with the Lord, you would be happy!"

Thus, we are led to believe that all physical and emotional problems have a spiritual cause. It's interesting how we tend to blame God for what we don't understand, or base all of our problems on a spiritual cause.

Now I am not saying that sin can't be a cause, but I believe that the cause is usually something more tangible. And there are other causes for emotional problems.

Two Kinds of Emotions

There are only two kinds of emotions. All emotions are either (a) positive or (b) negative. If we were somehow able to keep track of a person's emotions and put each emotion into a positive or negative column, the negative column would be the big winner with the majority of Christians. How tragic!

Emotions are simply feelings that are stimulated by the mental and/or physical parts of our body. However, these emotions are so powerful that they affect our lives and those around us probably more than anyone realizes.

Positive Emotions

When we feel joy or love or happiness or peace or contentment, which are all positive emotions, there is a radiation of pleasant influences throughout the body and even to those around us. These positive emotions have a positive effect on the functioning of our whole being, even to the promotion of good physical health.

But which comes first, the chicken or the egg? As Christians, the answer to that question is easy: the chicken, because God created everything whole. In the case of emotions, which comes first: the positive emotion producing a healthy body, or a healthy body producing a healthy, positive mind? In the majority of cases, the overwhelming evidence favors the latter, but not always.

Personal Experience

In my own experience, I found that as my body responded physically to my new lifestyle and I became physically stronger, my emotions became more positive. And I must confess that my thinking had degenerated to a very low state before I changed my lifestyle.

So I found, personally, that my poor diet and lack of vigorous exercise resulted in negative thinking. When I changed my diet and started daily, vigorous exercise, taking into my lungs copious amounts of oxygen, my body started to heal, and my emotions became increasingly more positive.

In fact, when I do my jogging, I often experience what some would call a mild *high*, a state of euphoria and well-being. I have also found that during jogging my mental faculties become very keen and I can do some of my clearest thinking and best decision-making. Nutritional doctors tell us that one of the greatest antidepressants available is vigorous exercise.

Negative Emotions

A body that is not functioning properly, whether due to a cold, headache, or more serious physical problem, will tend to lead a person to experience negative emotions.

The problem then compounds itself. These physical problems produce negative emotions. The negative emotions rob valuable energy from the body, which hinders the body's effort to cleanse and heal itself. Because the body is hindered in its cleansing and healing efforts, the stress produces more negative emotions. This vicious cycle snowballs and the results can be devastating. Sadly, there are multitudes of Christians who find themselves in such a predicament.

Feelings of fear, worry, sorrow, hate, jealousy, anger, and the like radiate a negative influence throughout the body. They also radiate negativism to the people around us. These negative emotions short-circuit the normal functions of the body, thus harmfully affecting it. Our bodies literally run an electrical current energy, and negative emotions dissipate this energy.

Many Christians Have Emotional Problems

Christians have many emotional problems, yet seldom understand the reason why. And, when they are faced with an emotional problem, the tendency is often to blame everybody and everything else for the problem, usually refusing to accept that the problem is within—they are the problem.

Some people turn to drugs in an effort to escape from these negative emotions; yes, even Christians. Some turn to the drugs that come in the form of pills in a little bottle. Some turn to alcohol. For some, temporary emotional relief may be found in tobacco, coffee, sugar, chocolate, or one of the most popular, constant snacking.

All of the drugs we learned about in Chapter 6 cause negative thinking and depression. If there is any relief, it is only temporary at best, and ultimately these drugs compound the situation.

Sugar is one of the cruelest culprits affecting the emotions, as it causes a malfunction of the organs regulating our blood sugar levels. High sugar intake causes the blood sugar levels to fluctuate excessively, sending people onto an emotional roller coaster. You might like to go back and reread Chapter 6 in this regard.

Negative Input

As to the cause for negative emotions among Christians, there is another side of the coin. On the one side we have physical problems producing negative emotions. On the other side we have negative input producing negative emotions, which produce physical problems.

We teach our teens, "You will become what you hang around." What you read, what you listen to, what you see, all goes into your computer/brain and programs it with good or bad, positive or negative. What goes in is what will come out. Garbage in, garbage out!

The Bible says, *"Be not deceived; God is not mocked: for whatsoever a man soweth, that shall he also reap"* (Gal. 6:7). This is an irreversible law!

Soap Operas

For example, it is exceedingly difficult for people to maintain a positive and healthy outlook concerning romance and marriage when they feed their minds on the TV "soaps." In these soaps, husbands and wives cheat on their spouses; there is physical abuse, alcohol, divorce, and all kinds of sordid happenings.

What is the result of this negative input in the lives of the viewers? Multitudes of marriages have been affected adversely, even resulting in divorces.

Most of the television programming of today is negative. Many Christians feed on programs that feature violence, murder, rape, war, abuse, lawbreaking, drugs, stealing, etc. The average preschooler watches 30 hours of TV a week. By age 16, that child will have watched 16,000 hours of TV compared to only 12,000 hours in school. This amount of negative input can do incalculable harm.

The words of many of the songs of today promote the negative, including drugs, alcohol, and unfaithfulness. Even the newscasts seem always to feature the negative events of the world.

What Can Christians Do?

Any Christian who wants to live a happy, abundant Christian life must shun as many negative inputs as possible. Why? Because these negative inputs produce negative thinking, which produces an unhappy person and disastrously affects his life, his future, and all with whom he comes in contact.

These negative thoughts and feelings also have a negative effect on the body and short-circuit its operation. Negative emotions, stress, and depression can create many physical problems.

Excessive Negative Input in the Church

Before concluding this chapter, I would like to touch on an area that has become an increasing concern to me the longer I am involved in the Lord's work. That is excessive negative input in our churches. And remember, this is coming from a preacher.

When I was in school preparing for the ministry, we had a guest speaker who spoke to us "preacher boys." The main thrust of his message was, "If you want to be a great preacher and build a big church, you must preach against things! It doesn't matter what it is, just preach against it."

This particular message left a very deep impression on me; so much so, that it became the major approach in my preaching for many, many years. But as time went by, I was less and less pleased with the product that this type of approach was producing in the people to whom I ministered.

Now certainly, as Christians, we must be against things— Jesus was! But we must not be so obsessed with the negative that we relegate the positive to a secondary position or eliminate it altogether. We must not be guilty of encouraging negative thinking.

The Gospel—A Positive Message

The gospel message is a positive message:

1. God loves us (see John 3:16).

2. Jesus paid man's sin debt on the old rugged cross (see 1 Pet. 2:24). Jesus died, was buried, but rose again (see 1 Cor. 15:3-4).

3. Jesus forgives and saves sinners when they believe the gospel message and personally ask Jesus into their hearts to be their Savior (see John 1:12; Col. 2:13).

4. The Holy Spirit comes to dwell within each believer, guiding him in his daily life (see 1 Cor. 3:16; John 16:13).

5. Christians are assured that Heaven is their final destination at the end of this life (see 2 Cor. 5:8).

6. Jesus is coming again to take Christians to their heavenly home. "For the Lord Himself shall descend from heaven with a shout, with the voice of the archangel, and with the trump of God; and the dead in Christ shall rise first: then we which are alive and remain shall be caught up together with them in the clouds, to meet the Lord in the air: and so shall we ever be with the Lord. Wherefore comfort one another with these words" (1 Thess. 4:16-18).

That is a positive message from beginning to end. Christians ought to be the happiest people on earth. Christians personally know the Creator. They know where they came from. They know why they are here. They know where they are going when this life is over!

Needed: A Positive Christianity

How desperately we need a positive approach to Christianity, from every pastor, church worker, and Christian. Too often it seems that Christians have a gloom-and-doom complex and it has produced many emotional and physical problems. My brethren, these things ought not so to be!

Many people in the world have shunned Christianity because they think it is only a religion of don'ts and many of the Christians with whom they come in contact are anything but positive and happy. The world needs to see a consistent, positive Christianity. Christians need to accentuate the positive for their own mental and physical well-being, as well as to show a negative old world something different. Something better!

Christians ought to be the healthiest and happiest people on the face of this earth!

Chapter 8—In Review

1. Many Christians experience emotional problems.

2. There are only two kinds of emotions—positive and negative.

3. Positive emotions contribute to happiness and health.

4. Negative emotions produce unhappiness and physical problems.

5. Physical problems contribute greatly to negative emotions.

6. Drugs cause, rather than relieve, negative emotions.

7. Improving one's physical health through diet and vigorous exercise will lead to more positive emotion.

8. Negative input can also produce negative emotions.

9. We become what we program into our computer/brain. "*For whatsoever a man soweth, that shall he also reap*" (Gal. 6:7).

10. The gospel message is a positive message.

11. The world needs to see a positive Christianity.

12. Christians ought to be the healthiest and happiest people on the face of the earth.

CHAPTER 9

THE VIOLATIONS OF
GOD'S NATURAL LAWS

———≫•◦•≪———

*For by Him were all things created, that are in heaven, and
that are in earth, visible and invisible...all things were created
by Him...and by Him all things consist* [are held together]
(Colossians 1:16-17).

*And God saw everything that He had made, and, behold, it was
very good* (Genesis 1:31).

From the above verses we see that at creation, God not
only made a perfect creation, but also established natural laws to perpetuate this perfection. These were natural laws by which His creation would be governed. Without these
natural laws, His creation would not be able to sustain itself.

Natural Laws

An example of God's natural laws would be the law of gravity,
a law that we are all very familiar with. This law was established at
creation for the purpose of maintaining order and to allow man to

move about the earth with safety. If God had not established this law, life on earth would be chaotic, at best!

It is interesting to note that though this law was established at creation, man was not aware of the existence of this law of gravity until comparatively recent years. Did the lack of knowledge of this law's existence nullify the consequences of breaking it? Of course not!

Regardless of whether or not man knows of a law's existence, violations of that law bring a penalty to the violator. An example would be when a person gets too close to the edge of a high cliff and somehow falls off. This person may land on the rocks below and be killed. Why? Because he violated a natural law.

Likewise, the person who touches a hot stove will get burned. Someone who steps in front of a moving vehicle will be injured or killed. A person who, for some reason, keeps his head under water for a relatively short period of time will drown. These burns, injuries, and deaths would all be the result of breaking a natural law!

Natural Laws Are Impersonal

All of the above occurrences are the result of the violation of natural laws, and the laws that caused them are totally impersonal! Violation of natural laws will result in sickness, injury, or untimely death, whether the violator was a Christian or not, whether the violator was a spiritual Christian or not. The law will automatically be applied whether a man knows of its existence or not. Ignorance of a law makes absolutely no difference in the consequences of breaking it!

The Natural Laws of Health and Healing

God created man to be well and to have perfect health. God programmed man's brain to respond automatically to foreign matter entering the body, and He placed in every person from Adam and Eve's children right down to you and me, the DNA, the molecular basis of heredity, which contains the master plans for building the body, and the RNA, the cellular chemical activities, which enable the body to follow these plans.

When a person sustains a cut, the victim may cleanse the area or a doctor may put in some stitches to close the wound, but it is the brain that automatically sets in motion the healing process. Then we can see the miracle of healing take place right before our very eyes.

Most of us have personally experienced this healing in our own bodies and we can recall cuts, bumps, bruises, and burns we have had in the past that have healed.

Sickness Is Not Natural

The fact that God programmed healing into our brain is proof that God does not want man to be sick. When a person becomes sick, it is because a natural law has been violated. Period! There are no other reasons, excepting those we talked about in Chapter 3, when the sickness was for God's glory or because of sin.

If a sick person wants to get well, that person must stop violating the law that caused the sickness in the first place and start cooperating with that law. It is all so very simple when one understands God's law.

It is also very important to understand that sickness is the body's effort to heal itself and is just the manifestation of this healing effort. An example of this would be what we call the "common cold" that we talked about in an earlier chapter.

Other efforts of the body to cleanse and heal itself are manifested in fevers, swollen glands, tonsillitis, appendicitis, pimples, etc. When these manifestations are ignored or drugged or surgically removed in order to suppress the symptoms, the results will usually lead to a more serious sickness or even an untimely death.

Personal Accountability

Many people have a problem accepting personal responsibility for their own health problems. It is a lot easier to believe that some germ or virus or outside influence over which they had no control caused their physical problem, than it is to acknowledge that they personally caused the problem themselves. Often because of ignorance, people will even blame God or say that it is "God's will," thus once again, shifting the blame away from themselves.

The Bible continually teaches personal accountability. "*Be not deceived; God is not mocked: for whatsoever a man soweth, that shall he also reap*" (Gal. 6:7). And again, "*Know ye not that ye [your body] are the temple of God, and that the spirit of God dwelleth in you? If any man defile* ["corrupt the unity or perfection of"—Webster] *the temple of God, him shall God destroy* ["put out of existence"—Webster] *for the temple of God is holy, which temple ye are*" (1 Cor. 3:16-17). Read that Scripture again.

Health laws are simply irreversible natural laws established by God. In this regard, it matters not if you are a Christian or a non-Christian, spiritual or unspiritual. "*For He* [God] *maketh His sun to rise on the evil and on the good, and sendeth rain on the just and the unjust*" (Matt. 5:45).

If a person violates God's natural laws pertaining to the body and health, that person will personally reap the consequences of the violation sooner or later. It is inevitable!

The Body Can Take Great Abuse

In Chapter 2 we learned a little about the marvelous body God made for man. In Chapters 4-8, we saw some of the things man does to his body that cause him to have physical problems.

If the body reacted immediately and violently when we put something into it that was not natural or not good for our well-being, perhaps that would help. But often people ignore even the body's violent protests and reactions.

No doubt there are people reading this book who can remember the violent reaction of the body the first time they inhaled cigarette smoke, yet they continued to inhale that vile, toxic smoke. After they ignored the reaction of the body's warning devices over a period of time, the warning devices became paralyzed or deadened, until there were no more protests from the body. Now the smoker can puff, puff, puff his life away a little more with each cigarette without the body even offering any resistance—they may not even realize that they are violating a natural law, a law that declares man's lungs require pure air.

How the Body Manifests These Violations

Colds, fevers, headaches, stomachaches, indigestion, heartburn, tonsillitis, appendicitis, pimples, boils, rashes, body odor, arthritis, asthma, kidney stones, gall stones, cirrhosis, constipation, diabetes, heart failure, stroke, high blood pressure, obesity, pneumonia, tumors, varicose veins, cancer, etc. are all manifestations by the body of violations of God's natural laws.

God made a marvelous body and that is the reason it continues to function even after abuse is heaped upon abuse. The body continually makes the effort to cleanse, repair, and rebuild itself. This cleansing and rebuilding process was built into man's brain when he was created, and it has been passed along to every person born into this world from Adam and Eve to you and me.

However, no matter how marvelous a body God made, there is a point where the body cannot contend with or tolerate any more abuse and it starts to break down at its weakest point, usually the area that has received the greatest abuse or possibly where there has been an inherited weakness.

Cigarettes, Alcohol, Coffee, Etc.

For the cigarette smoker it is usually the lungs that break down first, although all of the body suffers from the use of tobacco. Sadly, this breakdown does not usually manifest itself until serious harm has already taken place in the body.

The person who consumes alcohol or coffee or tea or soft drinks will generally find the liver being the organ that starts to fail first. The cocaine and marijuana user will find the brain cells are being destroyed and those who smoke marijuana will also suffer similar problems to that of the cigarette smoker. In fact, marijuana smoke contains four times the tars and carbon monoxide as does cigarette smoke.

The sugar user will find the pancreas and related organs malfunctioning, resulting in blood sugar problems, as we talked about in Chapter 8.

All abuses or violations have a negative and destructive effect on the body. What are called *sickness* and *disease* are manifestations of the body's efforts to cleanse and heal itself. If the abuse does not stop at this point, the problem compounds and ultimately results in an early and untimely and "unexpected" death.

The Body Is Self-Healing

Earlier in this chapter we learned that there are natural laws for health and healing. We saw this natural law of healing in action when a cut, bruise, or burn healed itself right before our very eyes.

Most Christians, as well as many non-Christians, have violated many of the natural laws of health. I know that I was personally in violation of many of them for a good part of my life. As a result of my own violations, I had some very serious physical problems.

In the next chapter, we want to examine God's natural laws of health and healing. We will learn what these laws are. We will learn that, when observed, these laws will not only keep well those who apply them, but will bring healing to most of the physical problems that already exist.

Chapter 9—In Review

1. When God made man, He established natural laws to govern His creation.

2. God's creation was perfect and His natural laws were designed to perpetuate that perfection.

3. Natural laws are impersonal. They apply equally to everyone, Christian or non-Christian.

4. Sickness and disease are not natural but are the body's efforts to cleanse and heal itself after natural laws have been violated.

5. Each person is personally accountable for his or her own physical breakdowns.

6. The body can take a tremendous amount of abuse but there is a limit, and all abuses will eventually manifest themselves in physical problems.

CHAPTER 10

GOD'S NATURAL LAWS

FOR HEALTH

And God looked upon the earth, and, behold, it was corrupt;
for all flesh had corrupted his way upon the earth and God said
unto Noah...Behold I will destroy them with the earth
(Genesis 6:12-13).

Approximately 1,000 years after God created man, God said He was going to destroy His creation. Why? Because man had corrupted ("changed, to alter from the original"—Webster) the way God intended man to live.

Listen to the Bible as it again talks about man changing the way God intended him to live, only this time, it is after giving man a second chance. *"Professing themselves to be wise...*[they] *changed the truth of God into a lie, and worshipped and served the creature more than the creator...and even as they did not like to retain God in their knowledge, God gave them over to a reprobate mind, to do those things which are not convenient..."* (Rom. 1:22,25,28).

God's Moral Laws

Certainly all Christians are aware of how man has rebelled against and broken the moral laws of God. These moral laws are clearly set forth throughout the Old and New Testament of the Bible. They warn against murder, stealing, lying, cheating, sexual promiscuity, etc. But man rebelled against God's laws, went his own way, and did his own thing. For these violations, man has paid a terrible price.

Ignorance of God's Natural Laws

Most Christians are aware of and try to observe God's moral laws but what about God's natural laws—the laws of physics and chemistry? To most Christians, this is an unfamiliar area. Why? Because Christianity has devoted itself almost entirely to the spiritual side of man, while ignoring the physical side. Yet the Bible clearly teaches that man is a triune being, comprised of a spirit, soul, and body. "*I pray God your whole spirit and soul and body be preserved blameless unto the coming of the Lord Jesus Christ*" (1 Thess. 5:23).

Why Christians, even preachers, have ignored and even rejected God's natural laws, I don't know. But what I do know is that these laws are real, and violators of these laws, whether Christians or non-Christians, will pay a terrible price for these violations in needless pain, suffering, and premature death.

Personal Testimony

In previous chapters I spoke about physical changes I experienced as I applied God's natural laws to my own body, changes that were almost unbelievable and would be considered miracles by those not familiar with the way the body functions. Let me share a few of these changes that I personally experienced when I changed my diet and lifestyle.

1. My cancer either went away or went into remission. After 17 years I am not about to go to the medical profession to find out which.

2. My blood pressure dropped from 150/90 to 110/70.

3. My pulse rate dropped from the low 70s to the upper 40s at rest.

4. My allergies departed. These allergies had been so severe at certain times of the year, that I could not preach many a sermon without medication.

5. My sinuses cleared up.

6. My eyesight improved. I still have a pair of prescription glasses over 20 years old that are too strong.

7. My body odor and dandruff problems just up and left me.

8. Hemorrhoids, which often required medication, went away.

9. Since 1976 when I started applying God's natural laws, I have not had a cold, an upset stomach, the flu, a headache, indigestion, constipation, or any other physical problem. To God be the glory! His natural laws and ways of living work.

10. My physical capabilities have improved spectacularly. My physical endurance is boundless. At age 42 I would be out of breath from just climbing a flight of stairs. Now, many many years later, I can literally run up mountains.

You may want to reject what this book is teaching, but you cannot deny that the teachings of this book worked when I applied them to my body and life.

What Are These Natural Laws?

What changes did I make in my lifestyle in 1976 that brought about these physical changes in my body and in my health? What are the natural laws that God established to keep man well and that would heal man's physical problems if the violations were stopped before man was drugged, burned, mutilated, or died?

To answer these questions, we have to go back to creation and see what God told man and into what kind of environment God placed man, and we have to assume that the way God taught man to live in the beginning was the way God intended man to live always. *"For I am the Lord, I change not"* (Mal. 3:6).

Let's Take an Example

After God created man, *"The Lord God took the man and put him into the garden…to dress it and to keep it"* (Gen. 2:15). Then, after man had sinned, *"The Lord God sent him forth from the Garden of Eden to till the ground…"* (Gen. 3:23).

Here is what I am getting at…the further man removes himself from the way God intended man to live, the more likelihood there is that man will experience problems! Thus, rural living is closer to God's plan for man than suburban living, and urban (city) living is even further removed from God's plan than suburban living.

Most readers will agree with me that there is a greater feeling of closeness to our Creator while walking down a country lane, walking through the woods, or while working in the garden than there is in the concrete jungle of the city with its polluted air, polluted water, traffic jams, noise, crime, and rapid pace of life.

God intended man to live close to the earth so that man could *"till the ground from whence he was taken"* (Gen. 3:23). *"And the Lord God planted a garden eastward in Eden; and there He put the man whom He had formed"* (Gen. 2:8).

Man Should Live to Be 120 Years Old

If we want a healthy, happy, physically active life free from sickness and disease right up until death, about 120 years, barring an accident or the Lord's return, we must try to make these natural laws a part of our lives. The closer we observe them, the greater we will be rewarded with superior health and a longer life. As to the length of life following the flood, God said, *"His days shall be an hundred and twenty years"* (Gen. 6:3).

For the rest of this chapter, let's supply either the implied teachings of the Bible, the direct and clear teaching of the Bible, or the practical experiences and scientific knowledge of today to find out what God's natural laws of health are.

Pure Air

What kind of air would you expect to find in the Garden of Eden? Probably the best word to describe it would be *pure* air, loaded with life-giving oxygen being given off by the plants and trees in the garden.

The greatest need of the body is pure air. If we want to experience superior health, we must avoid polluted air. The greater the pollution, the greater the harm to the body. If you smoke, stop! Shun smoke-filled rooms or any enclosed area with polluted air.

If you live in a city with poor air quality, consider a move to an area outside of the city and away from the pollution. Whatever changes are necessary in order to have fresh, pure air to breathe ought to receive serious consideration. Your health and very life depend on an abundant supply of pure air.

Pure Water

Did God provide water for His creation? Yes! "*And a river went out of Eden to water the garden*" (Gen. 2:10). What kind of water did God provide? It would have to be best described as *pure* water. Certainly the rivers were not polluted immediately after creation. Today man has so polluted the earth that it is almost impossible to find a source of pure water. Even rain water picks up so many pollutants as it falls through the atmosphere that it is anything but pure by the time it reaches the ground.

Probably the best way to obtain pure water today is to purify your own drinking water right in your own home. Since 1976 I have been purifying the water in my home with a stainless steel steam water distiller. It does require an initial investment, but if we want our bodies and those of our family to be healthy, we must put only pure water into them.

The body uses water to cleanse and remove toxins, to lubricate, to cool the body when overheated, etc. In fact, the body is comprised of 75% to 85% water. For the proper functioning of the body to maintain health, to cleanse, or to heal, the body must have pure water.

Pure Living Food

"And out of the ground made the Lord God to grow every tree that is pleasant to the sight, and good for food..." (Gen. 2:9). *"And God said, behold, I have given you every herb bearing seed* [vegetables]*, which is upon the face of all the earth, and every tree, in the which is the fruit of a tree yielding seed; to you it shall be for meat"* (Gen. 1:29).

Food comprises only about 4% of the nutritional needs of the body. Yet without the right kinds of food prepared in the right manner, the body is incapable of building strong, healthy, vital, vibrant cells and maintaining the body in superior health. Eating the wrong kinds of foods or foods prepared in the wrong manner can create havoc in the body, clog up the body, and cause all kinds of physical problems.

So let's see what we can learn about the food God intended man to eat:

1. All men from Adam to Noah were vegetarians and fruitarians. In Genesis 1:29 God said in substance, "Fruits and vegetables, seeds, grains, and nuts; to you it shall be for food." On this meatless diet man lived an average for 912 years without a single recorded instance of sickness. You might find it interesting to read the first five chapters of Genesis in this regard.

2. Meat was not consumed by man for over 1,000 years after creation. It wasn't until after the flood, when all vegetation had been destroyed by water, that man began to eat meat. See Genesis 9:3. It is interesting to note that after man began eating meat, it took only a few generations for man's life span to drop from over 900 years to about 100. Genesis chapter 11 shows this rapid decline in

life span very vividly. The life span of man then continued to decline to about 70 years.

3. Food was eaten in its whole, natural, living, raw state. There is not one indication in the Bible that for the first 1,000 years after creation man cooked his food. Certainly they did not have gas or electric ranges or microwave ovens.

4. Food was not processed, packaged, canned, frozen, or irradiated. Nor were any chemical preservatives, coloring agents, flavor enhancers, growth hormones, antibiotics, etc., added.

This food was grown organically. There were no chemical fertilizers, pesticides, herbicides or fungicides used on the plants or applied to the ground.

In Summary

Man's original diet consisted of raw vegetables, raw fruits, uncooked seeds, grains, and nuts, which had been grown without any chemical poisons. This food was eaten in its whole, raw, living state without cooking, processing, or additives. Does this sound like the kind of food and the way the average person consumes his food today? Today by the time food is put into our mouths, it bears little resemblance to the real thing.

The question is not "Where's the beef?" The question is "Where is the food? Where is the nutrition? What has man done to the natural, wholesome food God created and intended man to eat?"

We have a body comprised of trillions of living cells. Living cells cannot be nourished with dead food. Life begets life! All cooked food is dead food. The heat of cooking destroys all of the enzymes, over 80% of the vitamins, changes the protein to an unusable form, and the organic minerals revert back to their inorganic state.

Tests conducted on raw eaters reveal that when cooked food is consumed, it actually causes the white blood cells to multiply in order to deal with this toxic, foreign substance entering the body. That man is supposed to eat his food raw may be the most difficult thing to accept in this book because the cooking of food has been practiced for thousands of years. It is a habit! Most of the human race is addicted to cooked foods.

Yet man is the only member of the animal kingdom that cooks his food. Also, except where man has tampered with its food, sickness is practically nonexistent in the animal kingdom.

In comparatively recent years, remote tribes have been found. They had been separated from the rest of the world for thousands of years and yet they were found practically free of sickness and disease. When they started eating the processed, devitalized food of modern man, they began having problems similar to the so-called civilized world.

Today, if man wants to experience superior health and avoid sickness and disease, he must consume his food in a state as close as it can be to the way God created it and intended man to consume it, without processing, additives, or heat, and grown organically.

Vigorous Exercise

God created man to be physically active because He put man into a garden setting that required physical exertion in order to sustain life. In Genesis 2:15, God said man was to "dress and keep" the garden. Genesis 3:19 says that in order to dress and keep the garden, it would require "*the sweat of thy face*." Genesis 3:23 says man was to "*till the ground*."

When God created man, He created him so that physical activity would be necessary in order for man to obtain his food, and that the physical activity necessary to obtain his food would be vigorous enough to cause him to sweat. The Bible even says "*that if any would not work, neither should he eat*" (2 Thess. 3:10).

It is only in recent years that we have learned that daily physical exercise is an absolute imperative to maintaining a healthy body. Yet man still seems to pride himself on how much physical work he can escape. For the body to function properly and in order to experience superior health, daily, vigorous physical exercise is an absolute necessity.

Abundant Sunshine

God created man to live his life mostly in the great out-of-doors where the body could receive abundant sunshine. In fact, man was created and placed in the Garden so attired that the sun would shine upon his entire body. "*And they were both naked, the man and his wife, and were not ashamed*" (Gen. 2.25).

Today the majority of people spend most of their lives indoors with possibly an occasional weekend or vacation outdoors. Granted, due to the depletion of the ozone layer, there is the possibility of getting an excess of harmful rays, but this is usually a problem only in the hotter climates during the hottest times of the day and year.

However, the body cannot function properly without sunshine. All of God's creation is dependent on the sun for life. The sun is man's best source of vitamin D. The sun makes it possible for the body to assimilate calcium. The sun supplies the body with energy. The sun warms and soothes the body.

Man needs to spend as much time in the out-of-doors in the fresh air and sunshine as is possible, exposing as much of the body to its healing, soothing rays as is practical and modest for the situation. Warning: If you have not been getting much sun, be careful not to expose yourself to too much sun at one time, and be sure to avoid sunburn.

Adequate Rest

"*The sleep of a labouring man is sweet, whether he eat little or much: but the abundance of the rich will not suffer him to sleep*" (Eccles. 5:12). The person who labors physically during the day will usually have little trouble going to sleep, and his sleep will usually be a sound sleep. However, the person who has little physical activity will often experience difficulty getting to sleep and often not experience sound sleep. Without daily, vigorous, physical activity, the body just doesn't function properly.

The purpose of sleep is so the body will have time to cleanse itself, recharge itself with energy for the next day's activities, and repair and rebuild its cells. The average person spends about one-third of his life in sleep. Sleep should be enjoyed! It should be in a quiet place. It should take place where there is an abundance of fresh pure air. The best place to sleep is outdoors, so the closer we can duplicate that condition, the better. Leaving the window open during sleep would be one suggestion.

As the person observes the natural laws set forth in this chapter, his need for sleep usually decreases significantly. This is due to the cleaner body requiring less time to cleanse, rebuild, and recharge itself. The quality of sleep a person experiences is often a good indicator of his physical, mental, and emotional well-being.

Positive Thinking

"A merry heart doeth good like a medicine: but a broken spirit drieth the bones" (Prov. 17:22). Thousands of years ago the Bible told us there was a relationship between our thoughts and emotions and the condition of the body. Today we have conclusive evidence that many illnesses are the result of our negative thinking and unstable emotions.

Negative thinking has a wearing-down effect on the physical body. Negative emotions can actually bring about physical problems. Negative thinking is one of the reasons why Christians get sick.

Positive thinking and a positive outlook on life are necessary ingredients for a healthy, happy, successful life!

Today's Society

The world in which we live today is very different from the world into which God placed the first family. Adam and Eve had a slow-paced life with few pressures and with lots of physical activity. There were no eight-to-five jobs, moonlighting jobs, or jobs that required hours of hectic travel. There were no electric bills, telephone bills, car payments, mortgage payments, or credit card payments due each month. There were no radios, televisions, or telephones to disrupt their lives, no traffic jams or sirens.

No, they were in a gorgeous setting, surrounded by beautiful trees, flowers, and vegetables, along with the beautiful singing of birds, gurgling water of the brooks, the rustling of leaves, and the singing of the wind in the trees.

The pace of life today is too fast, too hectic! Many people drive themselves to keep up with the Joneses or to have the so-called necessities or nicer things of life. God meant for life to be very simple, basic, and beautiful as man walked in closeness to God's creation. But man has made life very different and a lot more difficult than God ever intended. Man has corrupted God's ways. Man has changed the way God intended for him to live.

I have met many people living with an abundance of material things who were miserable and unhappy, while others who may have had little of this world's goods were living a full and happy life close to nature.

> *But godliness with contentment is great gain. For we brought nothing into this world, and it is certain we can carry nothing out. And having food and raiment let us be therewith content* (1 Timothy 6:6-8).

Concluding Words

Sickness and disease and physical problems are not normal! They are the penalty one pays for violating God's natural laws.

God intended man to enjoy life. "*I am come that they might have life, and that they might have it more abundantly*" (John 10:10).

God also wants us to be healthy. "*Beloved, I wish above all things that thou mayest prosper and be in health, even as thy soul prospereth*" (3 John 2).

It is very difficult to enjoy life or anything else if you do not have your health.

God provided a way to a healthy, happy, spiritual life. Now it is up to each one of us to accept God's abundant provision. *"If ye know these things, happy are ye if you do them"* (John 13:17).

Chapter 10—In Review

The best way to review Chapter 10 is to re-read "God's Natural Laws." They hold the key to your health, happiness, future, and very life!

CHAPTER 11

IT'S TIME TO DO
SOMETHING ABOUT IT!

—————— ❧ ——————

...I have set before you life and death, blessing and cursing: therefore choose life, that both thou and thy seed may live (Deuteronomy 30:19).

While writing Chapter 10 of this book, I received two letters that distressed me very greatly, and yet they so clearly reveal the importance of this book and the urgency of getting it into the hands of all Christians.

The first letter was from my sister, Carolyn:

Dear George,

I have the most terrible news anyone could ever have in their life. My sweetheart died of cancer. He was only 52. We loved each other so much. We had our new home and we were so happy. Around August, he began to act very odd. He became violent toward things and verbally abusive to almost anyone in sight, especially me. I was in shock. I was at a total loss. I couldn't begin to imagine what had come over him. I never dreamed of physical illness—he had a hernia operation July 10 and they said he was fine.

In September he developed sciatica in his left leg. Soon after, a pain in his left shoulder. Then on September 20, his left collarbone broke, just broke during the night! At the emergency room, they told us to see a doctor the next day. He went into the hospital. On the 26th, they told us he had cancer, the bad kind. They told me one year at the most.

Okay, we were ready to fight and do anything to prove them wrong. But we never had a chance. He had chemotherapy and radiation therapy. The pain was horrendous. It was heartbreaking! He was so brave. My emotional pain matched his physical pain. I treated him like a precious flower. He became so delicate, just like a skeleton. He was so dear. He would yell at me in my eagerness to help him.

Sometimes I was too rough, but then, instantly he would say, "I'm sorry. Don't pay any attention to me. I love you so much; you know I do." He was so sweet. I would have done anything on earth to help him. I never let him lose hope that he would get better.

On the night before he died, some man came in to see him and was praying over him as if he was going to die any minute. Frank opened his eyes and said loud and clear, "Wait a minute. I have other options? I'm getting treatments, you know!" He believed and so did I.

That night he was up and around. For the first time he waved to me from his window when I left the hospital. The next morning I arrived bright and early with the suitcase. He was coming home! But he was in a coma and never came out of it. His feet had turned black and his hands were beginning to.

I've never known how absolutely devastating cancer is. If only he could have had just one hour again, when he felt good and we could talk. But he never did from the time we found out. I would have given anything for that. Life and love are so precious. But there's no way to truly understand how precious they are until you feel them slipping away forever. This is the most frustrating experience imaginable.

I miss him terribly and want him back! But everywhere I turn, the door is closed and locked forever. He was so good! He didn't deserve this. We didn't. Why him, George? Can you tell me? Why did God do this to us? Please write to me.

How Would You Answer This Letter?

Here is part of my answer:

I just got your letter a few minutes ago. Tears streamed down my face as I read it. I wanted so much to be able to somehow reach out to you and try to comfort you in your great loss and pain. Life seems so unfair sometimes. Is there any way you could come down for a visit?

Carolyn, God was not to blame for what happened to Frank. In fact, the book I am writing contains the answers you are seeking as to why. The title of the book is *Why Christians Get Sick*, and it tells why Mom and Frank had cancer and why Dad had his heart attacks and strokes. I'm going to go into town in a few minutes and have copies made of the book and send one to you. This is just a rough draft, and it is not finished, but I pray you will find it helpful.

My Birthday Girl Dies

Just a few days after receiving the above letter from my sister, I received the following note: "Your birthday girl, Susanna, went home to be with Jesus, December 15, after major surgery."

Susanna was the daughter of a young couple who met and courted in the church. I married them. They later went on to Bible college and have been pastoring their own church for many years.

When their first child, Susanna, was born, her birthday was on February 12, the same date as mine. Because of this, Susanna has always been extra special to me! Now this beautiful 14-year-old girl was gone. The reason? In talking to Susanna's mom and dad, I learned it was because of an unsuccessful operation to remove a tumor that was pressing on her spinal column.

Some Cancer Statistics

1. Cancer is now killing more children between the ages of 3 and 14 than anything else.

2. One out of every three Americans will develop cancer during their lifetime, and this includes Christians.

3, One out of every five deaths in America is now caused by cancer.

4. Two out of every three families in America will have a member suffer the ravages of cancer.

5. Each year, approximately 500,000 Americans die from cancer.

6. What is the cost to the American people for cancer treatment? Over $100,000,000,000 each year.

Surgery, Chemotherapy, and Radiation

Dr. Mary Ruth Swope in her excellent book, *Green Leaves of Barley*, on pg. 21 states:

The uselessness of surgery for cancer has been known for at least three decades. Your surgeon, of course, will be the last to admit it. As long as he can find people to submit to his scalpel, he will! But, it is well known in medical circles that surgery causes cancer cells to spread.

Doctors at Kaiser Hospital in California have shown radiation to cause new cancers to form where the X rays of the first radiation burns normal tissue. Chemotherapy, too, is not as effective as we have been taught to believe. While it destroys cancer cells in the blood, it also damages healthy cells and generally weakens the immune system.

If Americans want to get well from cancer, heart disease, arthritis, diabetes, obesity, and a whole host of debilitating conditions, in my opinion, they will have to find non-orthodox treatment modalities involving nutrition and other remedies "provided by nature" as the major components.

We can't expect the medical community to inform us of "natural remedies" of which they themselves are ignorant.

Dr. Swope has served on the Foods and Nutrition faculty of Perdue University, and later served as Head of Foods and Nutrition at the University of Nevada, Head of Home Economics at Queens College, and Dean of the School of Home Economics, Eastern Illinois University.

Cancer Research

After spending billions of dollars on cancer research, the number of people developing and dying of cancer continues to rise. Deaths from cancer rose 223% from 1960 to 1982.

Recently, the American Cancer Society told us that research indicates an improved diet may be helpful in keeping a person from developing cancer. They make the following recommendations:

1. Eat more high-fiber foods such as fruit, vegetables, and whole cereals.

2. Include dark green and deep yellow fruits and vegetables rich in vitamins A and C.

3. Include broccoli, cabbage, brussels sprouts, kohlrabi, and cauliflower.

4. Be moderate in consumption of salt-cured, smoked, and nitrite-cured foods.

5. Cut down on total fat intake from animal sources and fats and oils.

6. Avoid obesity.

7. Be moderate in consumption of alcoholic beverages.

Heart Attacks

Heart disease is the cause of one out of every two deaths in America; over 1,000,000 persons each year. The cost to the American people is over $7,000,000,000 (7 billion dollars) annually. Recent statistics indicate a slight decline in the percentage of deaths caused by heart attacks. We are told that the reason for the slight decrease is improved diet!

I find this all very interesting. Why? Because the *authorities* have been telling us for years that what we eat has nothing to do with our physical well-being and now they are advising that a change in our diet will help reduce the risk of cancer and heart attacks.

Dietary Goals for the United States

In 1977 the United States Senate issued *Dietary Goals for the United States*. In the Foreword of this report, Senator George McGovern, Chairman of the Select Committee on Nutrition and Human Needs, said, "The purpose of this report is to point out that the eating patterns of this century represent as critical a public concern as any now before us."

Senator Charles H. Percy, Ranking Minority Member, said, "Without government and industry commitments to good nutrition, the American people will continue to eat themselves to poor health."

The goals of the report "suggest the following changes in food selection and preparation:"

1. Increase consumption of fruits and vegetables and whole grains.

2. Decrease consumption of meat and increase the consumption of poultry and fish.

3. Decrease consumption of foods high in fat and particularly substitute polyunsaturated fat for saturated fat.

4. Substitute nonfat milk for whole milk.

5. Decrease consumption of butterfat, eggs, and other high cholesterol sources.

6. Decrease consumption of sugar and foods high in sugar content.

7. Decrease consumption of salt and foods high in salt content.

The following is a statement of Senator George McGovern on the publication of *Dietary Goals for the United States* (Press conference, January 14, 1977, Room 457, Dirkson Senate Office Building):

Good morning!

The purpose of this press conference is to release a nutrition committee study entitled *Dietary Goals for the United States*, and to explain why we need such a report.

I should note from the outset that this is the first comprehensive statement by any branch of the Federal government on risk factors in the American diet.

The simple fact is that our diets have changed radically within the last 50 years, with great and often very harmful effects on our health. These dietary changes represent as great a threat to public health as smoking. Too much fat, too much sugar and salt, can be and are linked directly to heart disease, cancer, obesity, and stroke, among other killer diseases. In all, six of the ten leading causes of death in the United States have been linked to our diet.

Those of us within government have an obligation to acknowledge this. The public wants some guidance, wants to know the truth, and hopefully today we can lay the cornerstone for the building of better health for all Americans, through better nutrition.

The following is a statement of Dr. D.M. Heigsted, Professor of Nutrition, Harvard School of Public Health, Boston, Massachusetts (Press conference, Friday, January 14, 1977, Room 457, Dirkson Senate Office Building):

> The diet of the American people has become increasingly rich—rich in meat, other sources of saturated fat and cholesterol, and in sugar. It should be emphasized that this diet which affluent people generally consume is everywhere associated with a similar disease pattern— high rates of ischemic heart disease, certain forms of cancer, diabetes, and obesity. These are the major causes of death and disability in the United States.

> Ischemic heart disease, cancer, diabetes and hypertension are the diseases that kill us. They are epidemic in our population. We cannot afford to temporize. We have an obligation to inform the public of the current state of knowledge and to assist the public in making the correct food choices. To do less is to avoid our responsibility.

Here is a statement from Dr. Beverly Winikoff, Rockefeller Foundation, New York, New York (Press conference, Friday, January 14, 1977, Room 457, Dirkson Senate Office Building):

> There is a widespread and unfounded confidence in the ability of medical science to cure or mitigate the effects of such diseases once they occur. Appropriate public education must emphasize the unfortunate but clear limitations of current medical practice in curing the common

killer diseases. Once hypertension, diabetes, arteriosclerosis or heart disease are manifest, there is, in reality, very little that medical science can do to return a patient to normal physiological function. As awareness of this limitation increases, the importance of prevention will become all the more obvious.

And this is a statement from Dr. Phillip Lee, Professor of Social Medicine and Director, Health Policy Program, University of California, San Francisco, California (Press conference, Friday, January 14, 1977, Room 457, Dirkson Senate Office Building):

> As a nation we have come to believe that medicine and medical technology can solve our major health problems. The role of such important factors as diet in cancer and heart disease has long been obscured by the emphasis on the conquest of these diseases, through the miracles of modern medicine. Treatment, not prevention, has been the order of the day. The problem can never be solved merely by more and more medical care. Finally, our greatest bulwark against the interests that have helped to create the present problems is an informed public.

The Diet of Christians

For some reason, the average Christian or, for that matter, the average American has given little thought in the past to what they put into their bodies. Part of this lack of concern can probably be traced to faith in the food industry, believing that they would not produce or market a product that could be harmful, believing also that the government agencies set up for just such a purpose would protect them from harmful products.

American Medical Association

However, I believe that the American Medical Association has to shoulder major blame for the citizen's lack of concern. Their failure to warn the people of the dangers in the average American diet becomes quite understandable when one realized that of the

127 medical schools in the United States, only one-third even offer a course on nutrition, and that only one-half of that one-third require attendance.

When the *Dietary Goals for the United States* was published in 1977, the AMA in an April 18, 1977, letter to the Nutrition Committee states, "The evidence for assuming that benefits to be derived from the adoption of such universal goals as set forth in the report is not conclusive and potential for harmful effects would occur through adoption of the proposed national goals."

Before the end of 1977, the first edition of *Dietary Goals for the United States* was no longer available and had been replaced by a second edition. The second edition was published in December 1977 and contained a three-page foreword quoting the AMA who said that to change your diet may be harmful. The foreword goes on attempting to discredit the entire document by saying that science has not proven any connection between diet and disease.

Remember, this is all coming from the *experts*, the people who are supposed to teach and protect the citizenry; in fact, they along with the American Dietetic Association (ADA), are the only ones legally able to do so as the laws presently stand.

American Dietetic Association

And speaking of the American Dietetic Association whose members do have the legal right and responsibility to tell the American people what they should and should not eat and what constitutes a balanced diet, we find that their teachings are ludicrous ("meriting derisive laughter or scorn as absurdly inept, false, or foolish"—Webster).

To find a good example of the ADA's teachings, check out the meals being served at your local hospital, meals prepared by ADA-approved dietitians. An analysis of these meals will quickly reveal that they are so poor nutritionally, they would contribute more to a person's remaining in the hospital than helping him get well and be able to return to his home.

Check out the average school lunch program for another vivid example of an ADA-approved menu: pizza, greasy foods such as hamburgers and french fries, hot dogs, and sugar desserts are just a few examples of the typical menu. And remember, this is coming from the *experts* who are supposed to be showing the American people what constitutes a wholesome diet!

If I Seem Harsh

If I seem harsh in some of the things I have written, please forgive me! I only want Christians to be aware of the situation. However, neither Christians nor the American people will realize what is happening to them unless someone tells them and warns them.

If I have come down hard on the medical profession or the ADA, I am not denouncing any particular individual. Most are sincerely trying to help their fellow man. However, no matter how sincere, they are wrong in their whole approach to nutrition, health, and healing.

Thank God, He showed me the error of the teachings and methods used by these groups. But it is an outrage when Christians follow their pernicious teachings and allow them to drug, burn, and mutilate their bodies, bodies that are the "temples of God."

Christian Schools

For many years, Christians sat idly by and allowed a secular, humanistic educational system remove God, the Bible, prayer, and the teachings of morality from the classrooms of our public schools, while teaching that man descended from a monkey.

When the Christian community was sufficiently outraged, they did something about it and, thus, the Christian school movement was born. This movement peaked during the late 1970s, at which time, a brand-new Christian school was opening its doors for the first time every day. Today, in almost every community in

America, Christian parents have an alternative educational system to offer their children. Praise the Lord!

Healing Professions

For too many years Christians have sat idly by while the world took total control of the healing professions as well as the bodies of Christians, which are God's temples. Christians take their sick to doctors and hospitals where the entire approach to healing and health are mostly in direct opposition to God's ways. Christians have allowed their bodies to be drugged by chemicals, burned by radiation, and mutilated by removing the unhealthy body parts through surgery.

When the patient doesn't get well or dies, the Christian accepts, "We did all we could," as a valid explanation from the medical profession and then spiritually rationalizes it by saying that it was God's will. It is high time that Christians realized that the medical profession's failures are not necessarily God's will, nor has the medical profession done all that could be done.

Hippocrates

Hippocrates, the great physician of the fifth century B.C., is called the "Father of Medicine." He said, "Where there is love for mankind, there is the love for the art of healing."

This great physician taught that food must be taken in the condition in which it is found in nature: uncooked. He further taught, "Your food shall be your medicine and your medicine shall be your food."

It is sad that the medical profession has deviated so far from the principles laid down by its founder!

What Can Christians Do?

1. **Start**—Taking steps to improve your own health will be an excellent start! The natural laws, found in Chapter 10, contain the ingredients for you personally to experience superior health.

2. **Change your thinking**—Christians, including pastors, evangelists, and missionaries, need to change their thinking concerning sickness and health. They need to start questioning whether their present diet and lifestyle will produce sickness or superior health. A mind open to new thoughts is an absolute necessity, if superior health is to be obtained. It is not easy to change lifelong thought patterns! Ask the Lord to help you.

3. **Education**—Christians must reeducate themselves. Knowledge is absolutely necessary in order to make intelligent changes. There are many excellent books available. We must stop accepting as gospel all that the so-called experts are telling us. Remember that if there were no sickness, the *experts* would be out of business.

4. **Teach**—In the churches, pastors and Sunday school teachers must include in their teaching the proper care of the body, God's temple. Our Christian schools and colleges must offer courses that teach the biblical approach to the care of the body and curriculum must be developed for the classrooms.

5. **Change the Laws**—The AMA and the ADA have a stranglehold on the healing arts. A parent whose child develops cancer can have the child legally taken away from him, if he won't subject the child to the drugs, burning, and mutilation of the medical profession. The ADA is presently trying to get every other field that offers nutritional advice banned by law, and that would even prevent churches from teaching a healthy diet.

   It is presently a criminal offense to offer advice to a sick person unless you are a member of their elite associations. Present laws allow medical doctors to drug, burn, and even mutilate bodies and, even if the patient dies as a result of these barbaric efforts, it is legal. Find out what the laws are in your state. Send them a copy of this book.

Because of current laws, Americans have to go to a foreign country if they want an alternative to the drugging, burning, and cutting. These laws must be changed!

6. **Hospitals**—Churches must start their own *healing retreats* where Christians with physical problems can be offered healing methods that are consistent with God's teachings. As the Christian school movement spread across the nation, when churches opened their own schools, so must "temple retreats" be established.

7. **Doctors**—These temple retreats must be staffed by nutritional doctors and nurses who have been trained in the natural healing arts. Christian colleges must provide these courses and degrees.

8. **Hospitalization Insurance**—The insurance industry must extend its coverage to include alternative methods of healing. This would result in tremendous savings to the industry as well as lower rates for the people.

9. **Organic Food**—Christians must start demanding that their produce departments and markets carry produce raised without chemicals. If millions of Americans would make this demand, the pressure exerted on the food industry would make it happen. Already in California and some other states, some food markets are starting to specialize in organically grown food. Germany has supermarket chains presently doing this.

10. **Grow Your Own Food**—Every Christian who has the smallest piece of ground needs to have a garden! It is amazing, but true, that a garden of only 200 square feet with a six-month growing season can grow the yearly amount of vegetables consumed by the average American. Organic growing methods must be taught in our churches and schools. We must get back to the land and grow our food as God intended it to be grown. Through the growing of sprouts, the average kitchen window can

be turned into an indoor garden where organic food can be grown all year long.

11. **Organic Farms**—In close proximity to every city in America, we need entrepreneurs who will develop organic farms to provide chemical-free produce for those who cannot grow their own. In colder climates, the use of greenhouses could make year-round production possible. Granted, produce costs would increase, but this would be more than offset by better health, and money saved that is presently spent on nonfood items and medical bills!

12. **We must share our knowledge, burden, and enthusiasm concerning the proper care of the body with family, friends, and neighbors**—This book can be a tremendous tool to put into their hands. Especially must we get this book and knowledge into the hands of pastors, evangelists, missionaries, Christian school leaders, and other Christian leaders who have influence over multitudes.

Some Concluding Words

The food presently being consumed and the lifestyle that is being followed are slowly destroying the health and vitality of our great nation, including the Christian community. Various forms of sickness and disease are consuming a larger and larger part of our energy, time, money, and emotions.

Why is this happening? Because we have gotten on the wrong road concerning health, nutrition and the proper care of the body. *"For wide is the gate, and broad is the way, that leadeth to destruction, and many there be which go in thereat: because straight is the gate, and narrow is the way, which leadeth unto life, and few there be that find it"* (Matt. 7:13-14).

It is not necessary to continue down the road that leads to sickness, disease, and an early grave! By changing our ways, giving up the bad ways and following the natural ways God has set forth, we can enjoy the wonderful blessings of superior health that our Creator intended to be our portion.

We must reject the life-destroying foods and habits that are destroying our bodies by refusing to partake of them any more. Old ways must pass away, behold, all things must become new with regard to diet and lifestyle.

There is only one way to deal with our physical bodies, God's temples, and this is God's way! His ways are perfect! His ways lead to superior health and a happy long life. May this be your portion!

"Beloved, I wish above all things that thou mayest prosper and be in health, even as thy soul prospereth" (3 John 2). This is my prayer for you. May God abundantly bless you!

...I have set before you life and death, blessing and cursing: therefore choose life, that both thou and thy seed may live (Deuteronomy 30:19).

And Elijah came unto all the people, and said, how long halt ye between two opinions? If the Lord be God, follow Him... (1 Kings 18:21).

CHAPTER 12

CONCLUSION

The Lord hath done great things for us; whereof we are glad (Psalm 126:3).

The Lord has been very good to me! When I was 23, He showed me the way of salvation. I accepted His invitation and received Jesus into my heart as my personal Savior. By that time, 23 years of my life had passed without personally knowing my Creator. But on May 29, 1957, the great Creator became my Savior.

Almost immediately I became concerned for others and began telling them about Jesus. It wasn't long before I was in school preparing for the ministry.

The Lord gave me many exciting and memorable years as pastor; pastoring four different churches; starting two new churches, a Christian school, and a Bible Institute; spending 15 years as a radio pastor with the America Needs Christ radio broadcast, and much more. But the most thrilling part of it all was the privilege of sharing Jesus with others, seeing multitudes come to know Jesus personally, along with their lives being changed in such marvelous ways.

During those years, I often said when urged to slow down due to my zeal and total dedication, "I would rather burn out than rust out!" But when, at the age of 42, I found myself about to burn out, the prognosis for colon cancer is not very exciting, I just could not accept it as "God's will" for me and I started seeking answers. (In Chapter 1, I shared some of these experiences.)

Now, some Christians may question my emphasis on the body in this book, but I believe with all my heart that the Lord has shown me the things in this book and prepared me for a "Temple ministry"!

There are literally thousands of ministers helping to prepare people to die. But how many are teaching people how to live? How many are teaching people how to live a vibrantly healthy, abundantly happy life so that they will have the energy and health to share Christ, yes, even the health to remain alive to tell the good news?

Potential Ramifications

My Christian friend, do you realize the potential ramifications of the information contained in this book if these teachings were applied universally?

1. Missionaries, pastors, evangelists, and their families would not be forced to leave their fields of ministry due to sickness, or have their ministries ended prematurely by death.

2. Expensive doctor, hospital, and drug bills would be eliminated. In fact, the only need for doctors and hospitals would be to repair broken bodies caused by accidents.

3. Hospital visitation would practically become a thing of the past as there would be no sickness. Funerals would only take place when the elderly died from old age or as the result of accidents.

4. Eventually even nursing homes would become almost unnecessary, as the elderly would remain active, alert, and able to take care of themselves almost until death.

5. Through the teaching of proper nutrition and lifestyle from the pulpits and through missionary outreach, world hunger could be overcome.

6. Many missionary societies have used medical missionaries not only to help third-world countries physically, but also as a means of reaching people with the gospel. Think of the multitudes who could be reached for Jesus through a "Temple" ministry that not only makes the people well, but keeps them from getting sick. Missionaries could have a dual ministry, teaching people how to live, while preparing them for eternity.

My Personal Commitment

For the past almost 20 years of my life, I have been asking the Lord to show me why Christians get sick. He has done that and, in so doing, has also shown me how Christians can be well and experience superior health. The more the Lord opened my eyes and revealed His natural laws concerning health to me, the more I wanted to share this knowledge with others.

Several years ago, Dr. Al Janney, who was then president of the American Association of Christian Schools, asked me if I would be willing to set up a health retreat in Center Hill, Florida, where sick pastors, evangelists, missionaries, and Christian leaders could receive alternative health care. Dr. Janney had the burden and the facilities but not the financing. He tried to get other pastors to support the project as a missionary outreach, but the project died for lack of interest.

It was then that I realized that before such a ministry could materialize, the Christian community had to be made aware of God's natural laws of health and the need for such a ministry.

After spending several years writing *Why Christians Get Sick* and trying to place myself in a position where I could help others, I realized something. I can best help others by writing books, producing tapes, giving seminars, evaluating products, providing demonstration organic gardens and orchards, teaching food preparation and storage methods, and, of course, by being an example.

After several years of struggle, I have been able to situate myself on a 50-acre piece of mountain land here in northeast Tennessee, where there is pure air, chemical-free soil, abundant springs, peaceful surroundings, organic gardens and orchards. It is called Hallelujah Acres, a place where the beauty of God's creation is so abundantly evident.

My goal is to make Hallelujah Acres into a modern Garden of Eden, from which God's natural ways of healing and health will flow to Christians around the world.

Also I envision Hallelujah Acres being a place where pastors, evangelists, missionaries, and Christian leaders can come to seminars, where they will learn firsthand how to grow, prepare, and serve foods as God intended. Nutrition and proper care of the body will be taught and then these Christian leaders can go back to their respective areas of influence to share this knowledge with others.

I personally believe that the American people and especially Christians are thoroughly disenchanted with the present means available for dealing with sickness, health, and nutrition and are just waiting for someone to show them a better way.

I want to and am willing and ready to do all that I can to see this happen. Will you help me? I cannot do it alone! The job is staggering, but the potential reward can be fabulously exciting.

If you are interested in helping, please write to me. Even a letter stating that you are standing with me in prayer would be encouraging and appreciated.

Would You Like to Receive Our Free Newsletter?

Our ministry has grown tremendously in the past few years, and Hallelujah Acres is now publishing an extremely informative newsletter called *Back to the Garden*. And subscriptions are free! If you would like to receive this newsletter, please sign up on our website to receive them immediately at www.harces.com or write us:

> Rev. George Malkmus
> Hallelujah Acres
> PO Box 2388
> Shelby, NC 28151

Pastor/Missionary Project

Hallelujah Acres Ministries is establishing a Pastor/Missionary Project to place this book in the hands of as many pastors, evangelists, missionaries, and Christian school leaders as possible. The goal is that eventually every Christian leader will have the information contained in this book! If you would like to help with this project, mark your gift, Pastor/Missionary Project.

Are You a Christian?

Although this book is written for Christians, it is possible, dear reader, that you are not a true Bible Christian. If not, please consider that you can apply all the principles of this book and live a long healthy life, but spend eternity separated from God and Heaven. If this is your case, God's good news is that the Lord Jesus Christ shed His sinless blood as the full, finished payment for sin and was buried and rose again for our justification. By placing our faith and trust in Him and His blood alone, we are saved, born from above, become a new creature in Christ and headed for an eternity in Heaven. Will you place your faith in Christ now? (If you will, please write to me, and I will send you more biblical information to help you spiritually.)

BIBLIOGRAPHY

ABC of the Human Body. Pleasantville, N.Y.: The Reader's Digest Assoc. Inc., 1987.

Airola, Paavo, Ph.D., *Hypoglycemia: A Better Approach*. Phoenix: Health Plus, 1977.

____*Rejuvenation Secrets from Around the World*. Phoenix: Health Plus, 1977.

Allen, Hannan, *Homemakers Guide to Foods for Pleasure and Health*. Chicago: Natural Hygiene Press, Inc. 1976.

Berry, Linda, D.C., *Internal Cleansing*. Capitola, California: Botanica Press, 1985.

Boie, Thorwald and Shirley, *Raw Food Diet Plan*. Los Angeles: Boie Enterprises, 1971.

Bragg, Paul C., N.D., Pt. T., *Nerve Force*. Hot Springs, California: Health Science, 1975.

____*Internal Physical Fitness*. Hot Springs, California: Health Science, 1979.

____*Nature's Way to Health*. Hot Springs, California: Health Science, 1979.

_____*The Philosophy of Super-Health*. Hot Springs, California: Health Science, 1975.

_____*The Shocking Truth About Water*. Hot Springs, California: Health Science, 1975.

Christopher, John R., M.H., *Dr. Christopher's Three Day Cleansing Program and Mucusless Diet.* Springville, Utah: Dr. Christopher, 1969.

Cook, Lewis E. Jr. and Junko Yasui, *Goldot.* Yorktown, Texas: Life Science, 1978.

Diamond, Harvey and Marilyn, *Fit for Life*. New York: Warner Books, 1985.

_____*Living Health*. New York: Warner Books, 1987

Ehret, Arnold, Prof., *Mucusless Diet Healing System*. Beaumont, California: Ehert Literature Publishing Co. 1922.

Fathman, George and Doris, *Live Foods.* Beaumont, California: Ehret Literature Publishing Co., 1967.

Fry, T.C., *The Myth of Medicine*. Austin, Texas: Life Science, 1974.

_____*The Miracle of Living Foods*. Austin, Texas: Life Science.

_____*The Great Water Controversy*. Austin, Texas: Life Science, 1974.

Gray, Robert, *The Colon Health Handbook*. Oakland, California: Rockridge Publishing Co., 1982.

Heritage, Ford, *Composition and Facts About Food*. Mokelumne Hill, California: Health Research, 1968.

Hoffman, Debbie L., *The Raw Food Program*. Valley Center, California: Professional Press, 1984.

Havannessian, Arshavir Ter, *Raw Eating*. Tehran, Iran: Arshavir Ter Hovannessian, 1967.

Hunter, Beatrice Trum, *Food Additives and Your Health*. New Cannon, Connecticut: Keats Publishing Inc., 1972.

Jensen, Berhard, D.C., *Tissue Cleansing Through Bowel Management*. Escondido, California: Dr. Bernard Jensen, 1981.

Josephson, Elmer A., *God's Key to Health and Happiness*. Old Tappan, New Jersey: Fleming H. Revell Co., 1962.

Kirban, Salem, *How to Eat Your Way Back to Vibrant Health*. Huntingdon Valley, Pennsylvania: Salem Kirban Inc., 1976.

_____*How to Keep Healthy and Happy by Fasting*. Huntingdon Valley, Pennsylvania: Salem Kirban Inc., 1976.

Health Guide for Survival. Huntingdon Valley, Pennsylvania: Salem Kirban Inc., 1976.

Kirschner, H.E., M.D., *Live Food Juices*. Monrovia, California: H.E. Kirschner Publications, 1975.

_____*Nature's Healing Grasses*. Riverside, California: H.C. White Publications.

_____*Nature's Seven Doctors*. Riverside, California: H.C. White Publications, 1962.

Kulvinskas, Victoras, *Survival Into the 21st Century*. Wethersfield, Connecticut: Omangod Press, 1975.

_____*Love Your Body*. Wethersfield, Connecticut: Omangod Press, 1974.

_____*Life in the 21st Century*. Woodstock Valley, Connecticut: Omangod Press, 1981.

_____*Sprout for the Love of Every Body*. Woodstock Valley, Connecticut: 1978.

Lovett, C.S., *Jesus Wants Us Well*. Baldwin Park, California: Personal Christianity, 1973.

Lust, John, *Drink Your Troubles Away*. New York: Benedict Lust Publications, 1967.

Mae, Edie, *How I Conquered Cancer Naturally*. Irvine, California: Harvest House Publications, 1975.

McDermott, Stella, *Metaphysics of Raw Foods*. Kansas City, Missouri: Burton Publishing Co., 1919.

Mendolsohn, Robert S., M.D., *Confessions of a Medical Heretic.* New York: Warner Books, 1980.

Nittler, Alan H., M.D., *A New Breed of Doctor.* New York: Pyramid House, 1972.

Organic Gardening, April 1988, p. 59.

Parks, Mary June and Burgess, *Cooking for the Lord.* Frankfort, Kentucky: Park's Publishers, 1981.

Shelton, Herbert M., Ph.D., *Superior Nutrition.* San Antonio, Texas: Dr. Shelton's Health School, 1951.

_____*Fasting Can Save Your Life.* Chicago, Illinois: Natural Hygiene Society, 1976.

_____*Food Combining Made Easy.* Chicago, Illinois: Natural Hygiene Society, 1976.

Sherman, Ingrid, *Natural Remedies for Better Health.* Healdsburg, California: Naturegraph Publishers, 1970.

Swope, Mary Ruth, B.S., M.S., D.SC., *Green Leaves of Barley.* Melbourne, Florida: National Preventive Health Services, 1987.

_____*Nutrition for Christians.* Melbourne, Florida: Swope Enterprises, Inc., 1981.

_____*Are You Sick and Tired of Feeling Sick and Tired?* Pittsburgh: Whitaker House, 1984.

Szekely, Edmond, *Treasury of Raw Foods.* Costa Rica, South America: International Biogenic Society, 1978.

Thomas, Luke Gordan, *Dying at 60 Youthful at 90.* Tracy, California: Plains Corporation, 1983.

Tilden, John H., M.D., Toxemia: *The Basic Cause of Disease.* Chicago: Natural Hygiene Press, 1974.

Trop, Jack D., *Please Don't Smoke in Our House.* Chicago, Illinois: Natural Hygiene Press, 1976.

United States Senate Report, *Dietary Goals for the United States.* Washington, D.C.: Government Printing Office, 1977.

Walker, N. W., D.SC., *Become Younger.* Phoenix, Arizona: Norwalk Press, 1971.

_____*Diet and Salad* Suggestions. Phoenix, Arizona: Norwalk Press, 1974.

_____*Vibrant Health.* Phoenix, Arizona: Norwalk Press, 1972

_____*Water Can Undermine Your Health.* Phoenix, Arizona: Norwalk Press, 1974.

_____*Fresh Vegetables and Fruit Juices.* Phoenix, Arizona: Norwalk Press, 1978.

_____*Colon Cancer.* Phoenix, Arizona: Norwalk Press, 1979.

_____*Back to the Land.* Phoenix, Arizona: Norwalk Press, 1977.

_____*Natural Weight Control.* Phoenix, Arizona: Norwalk Press, 1981.

West, C. Samuel, D.N., N.D., *The Golden Seven Plus One.* Orem, Utah: Samuel Publishing, 1981.

Wigmore, Ann, D.D., N.D., *Be Your Own Doctor.* Boston, Massachusetts: Hippocrates Press, 1973.

_____*Why Suffer.* Boston, Massachusetts: Hippocrates Press, 1984.

Hippocrates Live Food Program. Boston, Massachusetts: Hippocrates Press, 1984.

_____*The Wheatgrass Book.* Wayne, New Jersey: Avery Publishing Group, Inc., 1985.

_____*The Hippocrates Diet.* Wayne, New Jersey: Avery Publishing Group, Inc., 1984.

INDEX

Our Featured Products

#201—Why Christians Get Sick by Dr. George Malkmus is very helpful in introducing Christians to a natural diet and lifestyle. Letters are received daily from all over the world from people helped by this book, with now over half million copies in print. *Why Christians Get Sick* is written on a solid biblical foundation with over 150 Bible verses. (Paperback, $8.95)

2-10 copies	$7.16
11-19 copies	$6.27
50 and over	$5.37

#202—God's Way to Ultimate Health by Dr. George Malkmus with Michael Dye has everything you need to know about how to return to God's original plan for nourishing the human body. Read what the Bible says about diet and how this biblical wisdom is supported by modern science and hundreds of real-life testimonials. There's also an entire section of recipes and tips by Rhonda Malkmus on how to set up your own natural foods kitchen. *God's Way to Ultimate Health* contains 282 pages of vital information that has changed the way thousands of people think about what they put into their bodies. Many people say this book has saved their lives. (Paperback, $18.95)

#203—Recipes for Life...From God's Garden by Rhonda Malkmus is the perfect companion piece to *God's Way to Ultimate*

Health because it begins where the theory and rationale for the diet leaves off. With more than 400 nutritious and delicious recipes, our prayer is that this huge 8.5-by-11-inch spiral bound book will eventually be treasured in every kitchen in the land. Healthy food tastes wonderful, and this book proves it! Has important chapters on how to feed children and young adults, along with menus and even a section on feeding babies. Detailed index lists recipes not only by chapter but also alphabetically. (Spiral bound, $24.95)

#266—How to Eliminate Sickness Video—This professionally produced 2.5 hour video contains much updated information not available in our earlier videotapes, including Bible Scripture and educational text. This is an updated version of the seminar Dr. Malkmus has delivered across the United States and Canada. It covers the basics of why we get sick and how to nourish our bodies to restore our health. It will change your thinking forever as to what is nutrition and what is not. *You must see this remarkable video or DVD!* ($24.95)

#231—How to Eliminate Sickness Audio—This two-cassette audio or CD was taken from the soundtrack of the above *How to Eliminate Sickness* video. This is a dynamic presentation of the health message from a biblical perspective. This recording has much new information not available in previous recordings. (Two tapes in jacket or also available in CD, $12.95)

#293 Healing for Life Testimonial Series—These DVDs let you see and hear for yourself compelling testimonies from everyday people who have successfully dealt with various illnesses and experienced a renewed level of health while following the *Hallelujah Diet* and *LifestyleSM*. Medical authorities also provide scientific facts that corroborate the guidance given in the Bible about attaining good health. Once you watch this series, you will feel the hope, have the faith, and know that you CAN improve your health—without toxic treatments! And like those who share their testimonies in this series, you, too, will believe that. *You Don't Have to Be Sick!SM.* Titles (Arthritis & Osteoporosis; Cancer; Diabetes; Weight Issues; Fibromyalgia & Lupus) available individually or in the 5 DVD set. Also available in VHS. ($21.95)

THE HALLELUJAH ACRES
LIFESTYLE CENTER

Embrace a new lifestyle! Spend five or ten days surrounded by nature, as your Health Minister™ hosts teach you about the Hallelujah Diet and Lifestyle™. Through practical experience, you'll learn to prepare food, eat as God instructed, exercise in the great outdoors, and spend personal quiet time in reflection and relaxation. Each center is located far from the hustle and bustle of city life, yet they're close enough to metropolitan areas for you to explore local attractions. Centers feature comfortable accommodations in houses designed in the style of their geographic location. Program price includes lodging, meals and activities. As we have many new centers opening, please call for exact locations. Call 1-800-948-4501.

Customer Order Form

WE SHIP!
Shipping Charges: $5.00 for all orders under $50.00. For orders over $50.00, add 10% for shipping and handling. Outside Continental U.S., call for foreign rates.
North Carolina residents, please add 7% sales tax to entire order.

MAIL TO:
Hallelujah Acres • PO Box 2388 • Shelby, NC 28151
Credit Card Orders: (704) 481-1700
24-Hour Fax: (704) 481-0345 • www.hacres.com
Foreign Orders: U.S. currency only, and please inquire about extra shipping costs.

NAME _____

ADDRESS _____

CITY/STATE/ ZIP _____

AREA CODE/PHONE _____ DATE _____

If using a P.O. Box, please also provide a physical address for UPS delivery.

If you are not on our mailing list, but would like a free subscription to *Back to the Garden*, please check this box. ☐

If you **DO NOT** want to continue receiving *Back to the Garden*, please check this box. ☐

Quality	Item#	Item Name	Price Each	Total Price

Method of payment:			
		Subtotal	
Check __ Money Order __ VISA __		7% Sales Tax (NC residents only)	
MC __ Discover __		Shipping	
American Express __		Total	

Card Number _____

Signature _____ Card Exp. Date _____

We appreciate your order. The lifeblood of this ministry flows from your purchase of the health-related products and books we offer. Every purchase made helps us to reach more people with the message that "You do not have to be sick!"…if God's laws of natural health are followed. Together, we are changing the way the world maintains health. Thank you and may God bless!

Additional copies of this book and other
book titles from DESTINY IMAGE are
available at your local bookstore.

For a complete list of our titles,
visit us at www.destinyimage.com
Send a request for a catalog to:

Destiny Image® Publishers, Inc.

P.O. Box 310
Shippensburg, PA 17257-0310

*"Speaking to the Purposes of God for This
Generation and for the Generations to Come"*